HOUSEPLANTS

A COMPLETE GUIDE TO CHOOSING AND CARING FOR YOUR PLANTS

HOUSEPLANTS

A COMPLETE GUIDE TO CHOOSING AND CARING FOR YOUR PLANTS

ANNE DE VERTEUIL & VAL BURTON

Macdonald Orbis

Acknowledgements

Special photography was carried out by Terry Long and Neil Wood, and Paul Williams.

The remaining photographs were supplied by:

A-Z Collection, Jon Bouchier (designer Lenny), Pat Brindley, Robert J. Corbin, Elizabeth Eaton, R. Elsdale, Angelo Hornak, Michael Leale, Michael Nicholson, Harry Smith, Spectrum, Peter Stiles, Michael Warren.

Art Director: Grahame Dudley
Typesetting: Peter MacDonald

Illustrations were drawn by Phil Weare–Linden Artists.

The publishers would like to thank The Geest Organization, Clifton Nurseries Limited and The Plant People Limited for supplying plants for photography.

A Macdonald Orbis BOOK

First Published in Great Britain in 1984 by Orbis Publishing Ltd

Reprinted in Great Britain in 1988 by Macdonald & Co (Publishers) Ltd, London & Sydney

a member of Maxwell Pergamon Publishing Corporation plc

Printed and bound in Great Britain by Purnell Book Production Ltd

A member of BPCC plc

ISBN 0–356–17567–7

CONTENTS

INTRODUCTION

There can be very few houses that do not have at least two or three plants in them, and most probably have a great deal more. This is because plants do much more than decorate our rooms – plants make them come alive.

Most of us feel the need to have some contact with greenery that is living and growing, and enjoy the sense of achievement that comes from watching plants flourish in our homes and put out new leaves or flowers.

If you live in a city and have no garden, or if the view from your windows is particularly dreary, then houseplants may be – or become – especially important to you as a way of making a garden within your own four walls, and one which has the added advantage of staying green all year round.

This book is arranged around an A – Z of 120 houseplants, some familiar, some less so, but all readily available from good nurseries, garden centres and plant shops. Details on the requirements of each plant are given, with information on propagation and particular health problems. The A – Z is intended to be used hand-in-hand with the more general sections on care and plant health, so that, for example, although an entry may suggest frequency of watering for a particular plant, it is worth referring to the general principles and methods of watering as well.

Large groups of plants with particular requirements – such as flowering bulbs, ferns and bromeliads – are dealt with in special sections, as well as individually in the A – Z. Other sections are included on displaying plants and choosing them for certain purposes and areas in your home, and these sections should be useful in helping you decide which plants to grow and where. It is not suggested that you should necessarily sit down with a book and plan your house planting as you might do with a garden. After all, people do tend to buy houseplants on impulse, or are given them as presents. One of the great pleasures of houseplants is that for relatively little expense you can buy an attractive addition to the home, and that it will be no great catastrophe if the plant does not survive. With some forethought, however, and a little research you can avoid any casualties by choosing the plants which will suit your purpose and adapt best to the conditions in your home, and this knowledge will be particularly important when you are buying expensive specimen plants.

Please do not be put off by all the *dos* and *don'ts* that seem to be associated with caring for houseplants. As with any kind of gardening, these are purely practical points related to what plants need in order to grow and stay healthy. Where houseplants differ from hardy garden plants is that they are mainly tropical or warm climate plants, grown in the confined space of a pot, and in an artificial environment. They are therefore far more at your mercy.

Although some will require more attention than others, all the plants listed in the A – Z section can be grown in ordinary house conditions. And once you know what a particular plant needs, most of the health problems need never arise, as they are almost always related to incorrect treatment or inadequate care. If a plant is showing obvious signs of distress or is simply not thriving, check the charts on pages 120-123 to see if the symptoms and remedial treatment are included there. For further information refer to the entry in the A – Z section of the book.

Once you understand how plants work and why they have certain requirements, then there is no better advice than simply to enjoy growing them. Talk encouragingly to them, play them music by all means; the simple truth is that plants that are appreciated will be cared for, and consequently they will flourish and give you constant pleasure as a result.

GROWING PLANTS IN THE HOME

No matter whether you live in a house, a flat, or a single room, whether your rooms are light or dark, warm or cool, or whether your taste is for the exotic or the familiar, you can be sure of finding plants to suit your preferences and your purpose from among the almost bewildering profusion of plants available. The real art of successful indoor gardening, however, lies in achieving a balance between what you want from a plant and what it needs from you.

PLANTS AS LIVING DECORATION

You may be very selective about the plants you buy and limit yourself to a few large plants grown as features, or you may be unable to resist any attractive plant you see and end up with them growing in every available space. You may think of plants as a form of interior decoration and choose them to give, or add to, a particular effect, or you may find yourself becoming fascin-

ated by the whole business of growing and propagating them. But whether your plants are part of an ornamental background, or have slowly and seductively stolen the scene and become the main feature, they will be decorative only as long as they are healthy and growing well.

Unlike the rest of your furniture, plants are not inanimate objects that can be dusted down and rearranged from time to time, and plants will show their displeasure, some more quickly than others, if they are treated in this way. Plants are living, growing things that need to be cared for and to have their needs met if they are to continue to look as beautiful as when you first bought them.

If when you buy or are given a new plant you are at all uncertain about what it needs, it is as well to find out something about where it comes from and the type of conditions that would be found in its natural environment.

WHAT PLANTS NEED

All plants need water, light and air in order to grow, and if completely deprived of any of these they will die. However, the relative amounts of water, light and air vary, sometimes considerably, from plant to plant, depending on the climate and conditions it is adapted to growing in.

If you buy a filmy green fern from a nursery or garden centre, where it has been growing in moist humid conditions, and put it on your windowsill above a hot radiator because it looks rather stunning there, then you will find it looking anything but green and filmy in a week's time.

SUITING YOUR CONDITIONS TO THE PLANT

When you think that one room in an average house could well contain many plants from different countries, all growing in the same conditions, it is hardly surprising that casualties occur from time to time. And yet with a little care this could easily be avoided. If a plant is showing signs of ill-health, this is almost invariably the result of incorrect treatment, rather than some mysterious affliction.

A plant like adiantum, which grows in the humid atmosphere of a tropical forest, is clearly going to have very different light and water requirements from a desert cactus, which is accustomed to growing in arid desert regions. One will need shading from the sun and a high degree of moisture in the air, while the other will need an open position, sun, and very much less water. You cannot, of course, expect to simulate the conditions of a Brazilian rain forest or a Mexican desert in your front room, but there is a lot that you can do to make your plants feel at home.

Warmth and light Apart from water, which you can easily supply, there are two other main considerations which can be vital to your plants' well-being and which will influence where you grow them. These are whether your rooms are heated or unheated, and whether they get any sunlight or remain in the shade.

Most of the plants we grow in our homes come from the tropical or sub-tropical regions of the world, and are not outdoor-hardy in northern climates. These plants can be grown as houseplants because most homes are able to offer them an artificially controlled environment which approximates what the plants are used to in terms of temperature.

Since many of these plants are jungle or forest plants, and are therefore adapted to growing in filtered sunlight, the light factor is not so critical and, unless you live in impenetrably dark conditions, sun, or the lack of it, need not be a problem.

There are some plants, pelargonium and coleus among them, which enjoy direct sun, but the majority of foliage plants will be happiest in conditions of good direct or indirect light – that is, respectively nearer to or further away from, the source of light.

If your rooms are really dark, then you will have to be more discriminating about the plants you grow, but the many beautiful ferns, as well as most palms, aspidistra and philodendrons will all tolerate quite heavy shade. Many plants will also grow well in good artificial light.

Similarly, unless your house is unheated, or particularly cold, you will still be able to grow most houseplants. Many of them, especially those from the temperate zones, will tolerate surprisingly cool conditions, provided they are not neglected in other respects. But assuming that you do not live in extremes of cold or dark, you should be able to grow a wide number of beautiful and interesting plants without too many problems.

If you live in a house or flat, there will be some rooms, usually the main living rooms and the kitchen, which are warmer than others. Bedrooms are generally cooler, and halls and passages cooler still. Bathrooms often represent a sort of halfway house, hot and steamy at times, cool or cold at others. This overall range gives you plenty of scope for growing a wide variety of plants with different requirements. Even within the confines of a single room, particularly if it is large or high-ceilinged, there will be some areas which are warmer or cooler than others.

It is mainly the widespread introduction of central heating into our homes which has enabled us to turn our rooms into dwelling places for plants as dissimilar in their appearance and habit of growing as the graceful weeping fig *Ficus benjamina*, the spectacular caladiums with their huge, colourful papery leaves, the exotic palm-like dracaenas, and the feathery hanging ferns. With constant warmth we are able to persuade the flamboyant bromeliads to flower, and have hippeastrums blooming in winter as well as our own hardy spring-flowering bulbs.

As we have seen, warmth is as essential to these plants as light and water, but even warmth can have its problems. Most plants will grow happily in temperatures between 18 and 20°C (64-70°F), but they may begin to suffer in temperatures over 24°C (75°F), particularly if the air is dry and the atmosphere stuffy. This, along with the tendency to water copiously and indiscriminately in compensation, is probably the most common cause of plant death in homes with central heating. Plants obviously do need to be watered more frequently if they are growing in constantly high temperatures, but they will rapidly succumb to a combination of soggy roots and dry leaves.

Humidity Most of the tropical plants like, and some insist on, a degree of humidity in the air. Regular misting of the leaves may prove sufficient, or it may involve keeping the pots of plants like ferns, marantas and others immersed in a larger container filled with moist peat or sphagnum moss. Plants like fittonias and peperomias, on the other hand, need a constant degree of humidity which is difficult to attain in house conditions, and plants in this category are best kept in a controlled environment in miniature, such as a bottle garden or terrarium (see page 132).

Other ways of alleviating general dryness in the air are by using humidifiers over radiators, or by standing a bowl of water near them. Those plants that dislike water on their foliage can be helped by spraying the air around them.

*Many homes have a fireplace that is no longer used for fires, and
this makes an excellent showcase for a display of living plants*

Summer and winter Another important consideration is that many plants need two different sets of conditions – one in spring and summer when they are actively growing or in flower, and another in the winter when they are resting or growing less. This applies particularly to the desert cacti, which must have cool, dry winter conditions if they are to flower well. In addition, palms, ficus, hedera and yucca all do better if they are kept cooler and drier in winter.

Unfortunately, it is generally in winter that these plants are subjected to the blasts of hot air that we need to keep us warm. A healthy winter-flowering azalea or cyclamen bought in bud may wilt and collapse within days in this kind of atmosphere, and these and other plants needing cooler conditions are best kept out of the main living rooms and in bedrooms or halls, provided they are not subjected to draughts.

You may wonder, after all this, whether it is even worth considering growing anything but the toughest of houseplants, but there really is no particular mystique attached to growing houseplants successfully. The theory can offer general guidelines, but it can never be a substitute for your own observations and experience of how your plants are growing and adapting to their particular environment. The best advice is to get to know your plants and understand what they need and why, and if you treat them with confidence and consistency they will reward you.

CHOOSING THE PLANTS

Your choice of which houseplants to grow is likely to be a very personal one, based on their particular appeal to you and how you feel they will fit in with your surroundings. The question of space and of how and where you display the plants for different kinds of effects are dealt with in more detail in the section on *What Plants Can Offer You* (pages 136-140).

One important consideration, however, is how much time you can afford to give your plants. There is no doubt that there are some plants which are more difficult to grow than others and which demand more attention as a result. If your time is limited, or you feel unsure of your abilities as a gardener, it is probably better to be realistic and begin by growing a few of the many plants which are undemanding and do not require special conditions.

The chart on pages 110-113 summarizes the principal requirements of all the plants listed in the A – Z section, and classifies them in terms of how easy or difficult they are to grow. It also gives a general idea of the height to which a plant may be expected to grow in suitable conditions, and of its season of greatest interest, if relevant.

Flowering or non-flowering? The foliage houseplants will give you a reliable, year-round display of their green or variegated leaves in a huge variety of shapes and forms. The flowering houseplants, as well as some of the more spectacular foliage plants, can provide welcome splashes of colour against a background that is predominantly green.

Flowering plants may be easy temporary guests, like an exacum or a chrysanthemum bought in flower and discarded afterwards, or they may be perennial, demanding rather more attention if they are to be brought into flower again in following years. They tend to need more sun than foliage plants in order to develop their buds, and a cooler resting place after flowering is over. If space is limited, you need to take into account that there will be several months of the year when little or no visible change is taking place, and in this case you will be better off with plants like impatiens, or the shrimp plant *Beloperone guttata*, which flower for long periods of time. Alternatively, choose those which, like abutilon, the begonias and the bromeliads, have the added advantage of decorative foliage.

Which specimen to choose When you are choosing a plant, always have a good look at it to make sure it is a healthy specimen. The leaves and general appearance should indicate strength and firmness, with no yellowing or discoloration. Choose flowering plants with plump buds showing colour, and not too many open flowers. The soil in the pot should be moist, never soggy and never dry.

A warm, draught-free bathroom may provide just the right conditions for plants that love a moist atmosphere

FERNS

The ferns are a large and diverse family of non-flowering foliage plants which come from all over the world, and within this family are some of the earliest known plant forms still in existence. Some ferns are fully hardy, while others, from the tropical regions, are tender in northern climates and best suited to indoor cultivation.

The beauty of their fresh green foliage in all its variety of forms more than compensates for the lack of flowers and makes them a perfect foil for some of the more brightly coloured houseplants.

PLANT CARE

In their natural environment, most ferns are shade and moisture-lovers, and though this should be taken into account when growing them in the home, you need not take things to extremes. Avoid hot, dry conditions by all means but remember that few ferns will thrive in cold, dark corners any more than they enjoy standing with their roots in water. Keeping constant and balanced conditions is the secret of success with ferns. They should be grown in a position of good indirect light, such as a north or east-facing windowsill, and many of them will grow well in artificial light provided they get enough of it.

Ferns are generally equable about temperature and will grow in a range between 15 and 21°C (59-70°F), provided that this does not fluctuate too much and that there is a good level of humidity in their surroundings. Keep plant pots plunged in larger containers of moist peat or sphagnum moss, or standing, supported on pebbles, over shallow water in a gravel tray. Mist daily in warm temperatures, except for varieties which have particularly delicate, easily damaged fronds like adiantum and *Nephrolepis exaltata* 'Bostoniensis'.

Water plant compost to provide moisture rather than wetness since the roots easily rot in waterlogged conditions. If a plant has been excessively watered, it is a good idea to remove the soil ball from the pot, take some of the wet soil from around the roots and allow them to dry out naturally in a shaded spot before returning the plant to its pot with new soil.

The best potting medium to use is one which is absorbent, free-draining and acid, for instance, one part moss peat, one part peat-based compost and one part sharp sand. Pot on only when the plant shows signs of becoming pot-bound and then only into the next size pot. Signs that a fern is becoming pot-bound are yellowing foliage and stunted growth.

The plants will need weak regular two-weekly feeds during the growing season. Use a high-nitrogen fertilizer which will encourage a lush display of foliage.

Most ferns are at home in shady but not dark corners, and like constant humidity but not wetness at the roots

Some species of fern are true waterside plants, such as this fine specimen of Osmunda regalis, the royal fern

PROPAGATION

Most ferns can be quite easily increased by division of the rhizome from which the plant grows. Cut a section bearing a few roots and fronds and pot it up in a suitable potting mix in warm, moist, shaded conditions until it has become established. In the case of those ferns, like davallia, with surface-rooting rhizomes, pin the section down to the soil with a loop of bent wire. *Asplenium bulbiferum* bears small bulbils or plantlets on the upper surface of its fronds, and you can simply grow these on by detaching a pinna (leaflet) with bulbils and placing it on damp peat until the roots form and the plants grow on independently.

Propagation from spores, on the other hand, is a task requiring skill and constantly warm, moist, humid conditions. Ripe spores are gathered from the spore sacs – sporangia – on the underside of the pinnae of a frond and scattered on to a moist bed of sterilized peat in a tray or propagator. This is then covered with glass and kept in a very warm light place. Within a few weeks a green film, composed of many tiny prothalli should form. The prothallus is the intermediate stage in the fern's life-cycle; it bears both male and female cells which unite to form the sporophyte from which the fern grows. The whole process will take several months to complete.

SOME RECOMMENDED FERNS

The word 'fern' usually conjures up a picture of a graceful, rather fragile plant with arching fronds divided into small leaflets, like the maidenhair fern *Adiantum capillus-veneris* (see page 31), but compare this plant with the curious stag's horn fern *Platycerium bifurcatum* (see page 91) with its large leathery and glossy antler-shaped fronds which grow to a length of 60-90cm (2-3ft), and you will appreciate the very wide range of shapes and sizes which the fern family has to offer. Platycerium comes from Australia where it grows on forest trees, attaching itself by means of short, flat, sterile fronds which wrap themselves around the bark or a branch. It can be grown in a similar way in the home, wired on to a branch or piece of wood padded with sphagnum moss. Mist regularly, and water by immersing both plant and support in a bucket of tepid water. If rainwater is available, so much the better.

If you use a cabinet or terrarium for plants with differing requirements, aim to please the most demanding species, in this case Adiantum capillus-veneris, the maidenhair fern. Other plants are Sansevieria, Ficus benjamina and Begonia rex

Another unusual fern is the hare's foot fern *Davallia canariensis* (see page 56), whose furry rhizomes – underground stems – grow round the pot on the soil surface and hang down over the edge, looking like an animal's paw. This plant is probably at its best grown in a hanging basket, where its graceful, deeply cut, lacy fronds can arch over the sides. It is more tolerant than most ferns of dry conditions and will survive in temperatures as low as 7°C (45°F). Other good subjects for the hanging basket are the many cultivars of *Nephrolepis exaltata* with lovely, rather frilly and wide-arching fronds. 'Bostoniensis' (see page 82) is probably one of the most popular of all house-grown ferns. 'Whitmanii' gives a denser, more intricate effect, with feathery, much-divided fronds. All need to be kept constantly moist but never sodden, and away from draughts and direct heat which will cause the leaves to shrivel and fall.

An easier and most attractive fern to grow is the holly fern *Cyrtomium falcatum* (see page 55), sometimes known as *Polystichum falcatum*. This has dark green, shiny, undivided fronds, with tooth-edged, holly-like pinnae. The variety 'Rochfordianum' has larger pinnae than the type, but is a smaller plant, growing to about 30 or 45cm (1-1½ft).

Another fern with glossy leaves is the familiar bird's nest fern *Asplenium nidus* (see page 37) which has bright green undivided fronds with wavy margins growing out from the centre like a shuttlecock. Given optimum conditions it can reach a height of 1·2m (4ft) but it usually stays at about 30 to 45cm (1-1½ft) in normal house conditions.

About the same height, but altogether more delicate in appearance is the ribbon fern or brake fern *Pteris cretica* (see page 93) which is both easy and delightful to grow. There are many varieties, all with narrow fronds, usually divided at the end, sometimes crested or frilled. 'Albolineata' is a variegated form. *P. ensiformis* 'Victoriae' is a really lovely fern with slender, upright, fertile fronds which rise gracefully above shorter sterile fronds of dark green with a white central margin.

Finally, a charming small-leaved fern for ground cover in an open terrarium or in a pot where it can overhang the edge is the button fern *Pellaea rotundifolia* (see page 85), with small, rounded, leathery pinnae on trailing or creeping fronds which can grow up to 45cm (1½ft) long. Pellaea comes from New Zealand, where it grows naturally in dry stone walls and on rocky ledges. Being a 'dry-growing' fern, it will prefer conditions that are not too humid.

BROMELIADS

A large family of strange and beautiful plants, often bearing brilliantly coloured flowers, the bromeliads come from a wide range of habitats over Central and South America. They may be epiphytic, that is, growing on tree trunks and high up in the branches in lush, steamy rain forests, or they may be terrestrial, growing in the leaf litter of the forest floor, or in bare desert terrain and scrubland.

The root systems of these plants are small and often serve purely to anchor the plant to its support. It is the leaves which are adapted to take in food for the plant and which determine its form. Invariably arranged spirally in a rosette, the leaves vary enormously in habit, appearance and size: they can be erect or pendulous, fine and grass-like or fleshy and strap-shaped, while others may be so small that they resemble mosses or lichens. The whole rosette may be a tiny star no more than 7·5cm (3in) across, or a huge urn up to 3m (10ft) in diameter. In many species the central

A bromeliad 'tree' like this can be made at home, on a smaller scale

leaves of the rosette form a vase with a watertight base which acts as a reservoir for collecting rainwater, hence the common name of urn plant.

An interesting way to grow the smaller epiphytic kinds of cryptanthus and tillandsia is on a bromeliad tree. This can be made quite simply from a branch or an attractive piece of driftwood. The root ball of the plant is wrapped in damp sphagnum moss and wired on to the branch. The moss and the plants themselves should be sprayed regularly with tepid water and occasional dilute foliar feeds should be given.

PLANT CARE

Despite their exotic appearance, bromeliads are not necessarily difficult plants to grow, though certain conditions are needed to persuade them to flower. A position in good light is very important, with some shading from bright sunlight. Deprived of sufficient light, plants will be reluctant to flower and the leaf variegation on those plants with decorative leaves may become muted or even revert to green.

The flowering season may be at any time of the year, but it is usually between spring and autumn. Plants bought in flower in winter will probably have been artificially induced. To bring a plant into flower, you will need to give it a temperature of up to 29°C (85°F). During flowering and for the rest of the year, a temperature of 16°C (60°F) is ideal, though billbergia and neoregelia will tolerate 13°C (55°F). What is more important is a high degree of humidity in the atmosphere. Excepting those with a mealy coating on their leaves, plants should be misted daily and pot-grown specimens should be kept in larger containers packed out with damp sphagnum moss.

It is neither necessary nor desirable to give the plant compost a lot of water. The plant will absorb moisture from the surrounding damp moss or peat, but wet or waterlogged soil at the roots and base of the stem must be avoided as it can cause rotting.

In apparent contradiction to this, those plants with a prominent vase need to have

Some bromeliads have fascinating flowers, but it is chiefly for their rosettes of foliage that they are valued

it filled with water, rainwater if at all possible. The water is gradually absorbed by the plant and must be topped up regularly, particularly when the plant is in flower and the rate of absorption is faster. Once every three or four months turn the whole plant upside down, let the old water drain out and refill the vase with fresh water.

Because the plants derive nourishment from the air rather than the soil, a rich potting mixture is not needed. The most important thing is that it should be absorbent and free-draining. A mixture which contains a high proportion of peat, sphagnum moss or leaf mould, with some coarse sand for drainage, is ideal. Pot on only as necessary. Since the root system is small, a maximum pot size of 18cm (7in) should be big enough even for large specimens. For the same reason, bromeliads do not need a lot of feeding. A weak liquid solution of fertilizer can be added to the water in the vase once a month, or alternatively applied as a foliar feed.

PROPAGATION

As flowering begins the main rosette starts to die, but it will have sent up a number of small offsets at the base which will form the new plants. These are left on the plant for several months and treated in the same way as the parent rosette, which can be cut away when it begins to rot. When the new plants are about one-third of the size of the parent, detach them cleanly with a few roots and pot them into separate pots in their usual growing compost, covering only the roots and leaving the crown above the soil. Keep the plants warm and shaded until they are well established and then bring them into a lighter position. The plant will not flower until it has reached maturity, which in some species may take several years; others, like aechmea and billbergia, develop more rapidly.

SOME RECOMMENDED BROMELIADS

The most familiar of the bromeliads must be *Aechmea fasciata* (see page 32), often sold in flower around Christmas time, and justi–

The earth star (Cryptanthus zonatus) is one of the most conspicuous bromeliads

The pineapple plant (Ananas comosus) can be grown from a bought fruit

Vriesia splendens gets its name 'flaming sword' from the lurid red flower spike

Cryptanthus likes to have constantly moist leaves, like many bromeliads

fiably popular for its long-lasting, carmine-pink bracts and silvery leaves. Remember that this plant, like all other bromeliads bought in flower, will have a limited life-span, since the onset of flowering marks the death of the original plant, though it may be many months before the leaves show visible signs of deterioration. Rather than discarding the plant, it is well worth

propagating as outlined above. Somewhat easier plants to grow and bring into flower in ordinary house conditions are the bill-bergias (see page 42), with graceful grass-like leaves and pendulous flower heads on long stems.

Ananas comosus 'Variegatus' is the varie-gated form of the edible pineapple plant *A. comosus*. It has green and cream striped

leaves, and the whole centre of the rosette is flushed pink at flowering time. The flower-ing bracts coalesce to form the fruit, but you need very warm humid conditions, up to 32°C (90°F), to achieve this.

The vriesias are grown as often for their leaves as for their flowers. *V. splendens* (see page 108) has dark green leaves, with pur-ple cross-bands; *V. fenestralis* has light green leaves with a tracery of dark green and purple, while *V. hieroglyphica* has yellow-green leaves etched with intricate markings in purple.

Guzmania (see page 70) has large ros-ettes of handsome glossy leaves and bold, dramatically flowering heads which can last for several months. Neoregelia and nidu-larium are rather different in appearance, with more flattened rosettes and stemless flowers which develop and remain within the centre of the plant, rising just above the water level in the vase. Of the two, nidularium is the more difficult to grow since it needs constant warmth and a high degree of humidity.

With the growth of interest in bromeli-ads and the idea of the bromeliad tree as a way of displaying the plants as in their natural environment, the tillandsias – air plants – are fast gaining popularity. They are an enormously varied group: at one end of the range there is the more typical *T. lindeniana*, with narrow, arching leaves and an impressive flower spike, like a flattened cock's comb, composed of carmine-pink bracts enclosing brilliant blue flowers. At the other end there is the strange Spanish moss *T. usneoides*, which comes from the subtropical states of the American deep south, where its grey-green mossy tufts can be seen clinging tenuously to trees and wires, existing solely on moisture absorbed from the air. More curious still are the xer-ophytic (dry-growing) tillandsias – small, brittle, grey plants with tangled stems, ad-apted to living in desert conditions. Other subjects for a bromeliad tree are cryptan-thus: *C. fosterianus* is low-growing and spreading, with wavy copper-brown leaves cross-banded in grey, and *C. bivittatus* is only 7·5cm (3in) high and has pale green leaves with darker green stripes.

Tillandsia dianthoidea – one of the so-called air plants

Nidularium innocentii: white flowers emerge from the red bracts

Collecting cacti and other succulents is a fascinating pastime

CACTI AND SUCCULENTS

It is usual to make a distinction between cacti and succulents, because although both are succulent types of plant (that is, they have fleshy, swollen stems or leaves which are adapted to storing water and enabling the plants to withstand long periods of drought), the cacti have one specific feature which distinguishes them from other succulents. This is the presence of a small cushion or 'areole' on the plant structure, from which hairs, spines, flowers and, occasionally, leaves may grow.

In general, the cacti are also characterized by succulent stems and an absence of leaves, while most succulents have hard stems, if at all, and succulent leaves. But this is not a hard-and-fast rule and it is the presence or absence of the areole which will tell you whether you are looking at a cactus or a succulent.

Cacti come mainly from Central and South America and from the West Indies. The largest and most familiar group comprises the desert-dwellers, with fleshy stems, covered with prickles or tufts of hair and, frequently, brilliantly coloured flowers. A smaller and less well-known group comprises the epiphytic or forest cacti, which grow with their roots embedded in moss on branches and in the hollows of trees in the tropical rain forests. These have branching stems and include the flowering Christmas and Easter cacti, respectively *Schlumbergera* × 'Buckleyi' (see page 99) and *Rhipsalidopsis gaertneri* (see page 94) and the beautiful flowering epiphyllums.

The other succulents come mainly from Africa, in particular South Africa, but they are also found in many other parts of the world, growing in regions of semi-desert and scrubland. As a rule their main feature, when grown as pot plants, is the leaf rather than the flower.

PLANT CARE

While there are many desert cacti that are grown for their curious shape, their spines or their hairiness, and which in normal house conditions will never grow to the height at which they normally flower in the wild, there are many others which will happily flower as pot plants and which will give a dazzling display for months at a time.

Cacti are accustomed to growing in extreme conditions – indefinite periods of drought interrupted by sudden, heavy downpours and long scorching days followed by sharp, cold nights – and you will be most successful with growing and flowering if you give them similar conditions in the home, even though it may seem callous to treat them in a way that would kill most other houseplants.

In summer the desert cacti need a well-ventilated position in good light, where they can get as much sun as possible. Water and drain them thoroughly, but only when the soil is dry to the touch or the pot sounds hollow when you tap it. It is not possible to be more specific than this, since the amount of water absorbed will depend on the temperature in the room, and this will vary from day to day. In winter, move the plants to a lower temperature – many will survive at 4°C (40°F) – and withhold water until the spring. If you are keeping your cacti in constant warmth throughout the year, however, they will need some water in winter but will probably be less willing to flower; the more severe regime gives better results.

The other succulents need rather less extreme conditions, with some moisture in winter and a little shading from very bright sun in summer.

Coming from a very different habitat, the forest cacti should be treated more like ordinary housplants. They require more moisture all year round, particularly since some, like *Schlumbergera* × 'Buckleyi', flower during the winter. They also need higher temperatures, light shading from intense sun, and a degree of humidity.

The roots of all the succulents are small and shallow, and the main requirement of the growing medium is that it should be very well drained. Use an ordinary potting compost, with added coarse sand or grit, and charcoal; alternatively, use one of the proprietary cactus formulas available. Give forest cacti some added humus or sphagnum moss in the mixture.

Occasional liquid feeds with a high-potassium fertilizer, such as is used for tomatoes, can be given between April and September to assist with flowering. It is sometimes recommended that a small quantity of bone meal be added to the compost in spring or when repotting. Bone meal is a slow-release fertilizer which contains high proportions of phosphorus and smaller quantities of nitrogen, and stimulates flower growth rather than leaf growth.

PROPAGATION

Cacti and succulents can be grown from seed quite easily, using either packet seed or ripened seed from your own plants. Sow the seeds in shallow containers with a layer of gravel in the bottom and a sandy mixture, or suitable proprietary seed compost. Keep under glass in light shade at a temperature of 24-27°C (75-80°F) until germination takes place.

There are a number of other ways of propagating succulents, ranging from simple division of clump-forming cacti to top or stem cuttings of branching succulents, depending on the way in which the particular plant grows. Some produce small offsets which are easily detached and potted on. Others, such as the branching cacti and the euphorbias, have obvious joints and can be propagated from cuttings taken along these joints. Allow the cut end to dry out before inserting it in soil. Opuntia pads can be detached and rooted in a similar way. The small fleshy leaves of some sedums and most crassulas can be simply pulled off and inserted in soil. Unfortunately the only way of propagating columnar cacti, other than by seed, is to slice the entire head off, and obviously this will be done only if the plant

A prickly pear (Opuntia) can be propatated by detaching its pads

Schlumbergera is an attractive flowering forest cactus

is showing signs of ill-health at the base or has become too large for its position.

SOME RECOMMENDED CACTI AND SUCCULENTS

As a group of plants, the succulents have a marked curiosity factor and tend to rouse strong feelings, either of fascination or of repulsion. Once you are hooked, collecting succulents can become a rather obsessive hobby – the more you buy, the more you find you haven't got. There is an enormous range to choose from and some of those easiest to grow and most commonly available are listed below. The cacti mentioned can all be made to flower in the home quite easily and should thus dispel the myth that they only flower at night once every hundred years. If you are interested in collecting some of the more esoteric kinds, there are many nurseries that specialize in selling these.

Desert cacti (flowering)
Chamaecereus silvestrii peanut cactus
Echinopsis eyriesii sea urchin cactus
Gymnocalycium (many)
Lobivia (many)
Mammillaria (many; see page 80)
Notocactus (many)
Parodia (many)
Rebutia (many; see page 94)

Forest/epiphytic cacti (flowering)
Epiphyllum hybrids (see page 60)
Rhipsalidopsis gaertneri Easter cactus (see page 94)
Schlumbergera × 'Buckleyi' Christmas cactus (see page 99)

Succulents (leaf and sometimes flower)
Agave (many; see page 32)
Aloe variegata (see page 34)
Crassula (many; see page 52)
Euphorbia (many; see page 62)
Faucaria tigrina
Gasteria (many)
Haworthia (many; see page 71)
Kalanchoë blossfeldiana (see page 79)
Lithops living stones (many)
Sansevieria (see page 97)
Sedum stonecrop (many)
Sempervivum houseleek (many)

PALMS

Palms are not plants for impatient gardeners. They are slow-growing and often take years to reach their full stature, and consequently large specimens in particular can be expensive to buy. In spite of this drawback they are not demanding plants, adapting themselves well to ordinary house conditions and requiring relatively little attention. And, certainly, as a permanent decorative feature in a room large enough to accommodate them, there can be few houseplants to rival their stately elegance and the beauty of the fronds as they unfurl almost imperceptibly.

PLANT CARE

Palms come from tropical and Mediterranean countries, where they often grow in the semi-shade of other plants or trees, and although they will tolerate quite deep shade, most do better in indirect light with protection from direct sun. In the home give them space to spread out – stuffy conditions can cause infestation by red spider mite – and water regularly and thoroughly during the spring and summer. Some insecticides and leaf-cleaning agents are harmful to the leaves, and frequent misting and occasional sponging of the leaves will give them the degree of humidity they need and should keep red spider mite at bay. It is perhaps surprising that many palms will tolerate temperatures as low as 7°C (45°F) in winter and actually prefer to be kept cool and dry during this period of little growth.

A well-drained potting mixture is important – palms dislike water settling around their roots. Line the pot base with a layer of broken crocks and use a peat-based compost which has some added sand to improve the drainage.

Palms are happiest in small pots and do not need to be repotted until the root ball is literally pushing its way out of the soil. Because of their slow rate of growth, it is unlikely that they will need repotting more than once every two or three years. For large specimens a maximum pot size of 25-30cm (10-12in) is usually enough; after this has been reached, you can remove the top layer of soil from around the root ball and replace with new soil. Always firm the soil down well around the roots.

PROPAGATION

Unfortunately, because of the time and expense involved in growing palms as houseplants, the number of varieties generally available is rather limited. If you are interested in growing some of the less common kinds, you might think about raising them from seed. If you decide to give this a try, it is worth investing in a propagator, since the seeds need high levels of humidity for germination. Sow the seeds on peat and germinate them at a temperature of 27°C (80°F), certainly no lower than 21°C (70°F). Germination should take between four and six weeks. When the first leaf has developed and the seedlings are several centimetres high, pot them into individual pots and keep them at 18-21°C (65-70°F) until they are established.

SOME RECOMMENDED PALMS

Of those that are readily available, one of the smallest and easiest to grow is *Chamaedorea elegans*, the parlour palm, also known as *Neanthe bella* (see page 46). It may grow to a height of 1·2m (4ft), is faster-growing than most and generally more tolerant of dry conditions. As a small plant it can be grown as a feature in a bottle garden.

Equally popular, but at the other end of the scale in height, is *Howea forsteriana* (see page 75), sometimes referred to as the kentia palm, which will eventually grow to 3m (10ft) high. Very similar in appearance when young is *H. belmoreana*, but as it ages the fronds droop downwards, and it needs a good deal more space than the upright-growing *H. forsteriana*. These plants are often sold as well-grown specimens, and like many palms, they do not develop their characteristic forms until they reach maturity. Both need summer temperatures of 16-21°C (60-70°F) and a minimum winter temperature of 13°C (55°F).

Phoenix dactylifera, the date palm, can be grown from a fresh date stone. It will probably take a good couple of months to germinate and is very slow-growing at first, but after the first four years it grows more rapidly. It has large, stiff, rather prickly leaves. Far more attractive in appearance, but even slower-growing, are *P. canariensis* (see page 89) and *P. roebelenii*. Of the two, *P. roebelenii* is the more graceful, with arching, rather sparsely-leaved fronds, but it may be quite difficult to come by. *P. canariensis* has a more upright form and stiff spiny leaves and is slightly hardier than the other two.

A very charming small palm, with delicate arching leaves, is *Syagrus weddelliana*, a relative of the coconut palm and still often sold as *Cocos weddelliana*. It is not an easy

European fan palm (Chamaerops humilis)

plant to keep in ordinary house conditions, needing a high degree of humidity and temperatures of 21°C (70°F) in summer and 16°C (60°F) in winter. If you are going to try growing it inside, keep it in a position of semi-shade, mist frequently, water well and give weak liquid feeds every two weeks from spring to early autumn.

Quite different from all these in form and effect are the fan palms. It is an interesting fact that the distinction between the fan palms and the feather palms, like *C. weddelliana*, is one of hardiness. As a rule, the more feathery the palm frond, the less hardy the plant. The fan palms are usually found in Europe and the temperate zones and will tolerate temperatures almost to freezing point, but the feather palms are tropical plants and must have heat and humidity to survive.

The Mediterranean fan palm *Chamaerops humilis* has its leaves arranged in stiff fans held out on a number of long stems. It grows wild in Mediterranean regions, where it is usually seen as a multi-stemmed bush between 1·8m and 2·4m (6-8ft) in height, sometimes even higher. It is very unlikely ever to reach these proportions when grown in a pot, and is usually seen at a height between 1m and 1·2m (3-4ft). It must have good ventilation in summer and very low winter temperatures.

In this it is like its hardier relative *Trachycarpus fortunei*, the Chusan palm, and the only palm which is properly hardy in most parts of the British Isles. It is usually grown in sheltered areas outside, but can also be grown as a slow-growing specimen for a conservatory.

A fine Chusan palm (Trachycarpus fortunei)

BULBS

Bulbs grown as flowering houseplants are a delightful and inexpensive way to bring colour, and often fragrance, into the house during the long winter months when other houseplants may be looking rather drab.

Hardy spring bulbs, such as narcissus, crocus and hyacinth, are flowered indoors by the method known as 'forcing', which induces them to flower earlier than they normally would outside. Forced bulbs will not flower again inside and must either be discarded after flowering or dug into the garden, where they may take a year or two to recover before flowering again.

The tender bulbous plants from warm climates, such as hippeastrum and vallota, do not need to be forced, since warm indoor conditions supply them with the temperatures they need to flower in their own time. With correct treatment they can be kept and flowered again and hippeastrum, in particular, will last for many years.

BUYING BULBS

You can either order your bulbs in advance from bulb catalogues or buy them directly from any good nursery or garden centre, ready for potting up in the late summer or early autumn.

It is always best to use specially prepared bulbs for indoor forcing, since these will have been stored and treated in such a way as to make them ready for flowering at the desired time. These bulbs will be in a state of expectancy of flowering, so it is best to pot them up as soon as possible, or to keep them in a cool, dark spot until you are ready. A healthy bulb will be plump and firm to the touch, and will have no blemishes or soft spots.

Which bulbs to choose Among the hardy spring bulbs, the large-flowered Dutch varieties of crocus, *C. neapolitanus* (*C. vernus*), are easily grown either in soil or water, and come in shades of white, yellow, mauve and purple. Hyacinths, too, can be grown in soil or water and the kinds most usually offered for growing inside are the Dutch hyacinths *H. orientalis* and their derivations the multifloras, with large flowering heads in white, pink and blue. The earlier flowering Roman hyacinths (*H. orientalis albulus*) are also very suitable for forcing, with less compact flower heads in white, pale pink and pale blue.

Most narcissi need cool conditions to grow successfully, but delightful exceptions to the rule are those like 'Paper White' which belong to the tender Tazetta group and flower earlier than the rest. These are among the easiest of all bulbs for indoor cultivation, growing happily in soil, or water and pebbles. They need only to be kept in a cool position in indirect light until the buds have formed, and then brought in to warmer conditions for flowering. You can have a succession of these lovely flowers throughout the winter by planting up bowls at two-weekly intervals, between September and December, and bringing them in as they become ready, to replace those that have faded. Discard them when flowering is over. Other early-flowering narcissi should be forced in the usual way, but brought in to temperatures not exceeding 13°C (55°F) and always kept moist.

Tulips offer an enormous range of colours, from white and the palest pinks to deep purple, almost black. The early-flowering single and double varieties are the most suitable for forcing. They need at least 15 weeks in cool, dark conditions, since they are later-flowering than other spring bulbs.

Surprisingly enough, a hardy garden plant which is often grown inside is lily-of-the-valley (convallaria), in particular the large-flowering white *C. majalis* 'Fortin's Giant'. It is not technically a bulb, but has underground branching roots, known as crowns or pips. Plant these in October in a rich loamy compost, with added leaf mould, and sand for drainage. Either keep the pots outside with protection against frost, or inside in very cool, well-ventilated conditions.

In January bring them in to higher temperatures of about 18°C (65°F) and keep well watered. Plant them out in the garden in a moist, shady spot when flowering is over.

The smaller bulbs like snowdrops, muscari and chionodoxa need the cold and do not respond well to forcing. Grow them in very cool conditions inside or plant them in pots outside and bring them in when they are about to flower.

For growing details of tender bulbous plants see *Clivia miniata* (page 49), *Hippeastrum* (page 74), and *Lilium longiflorum* (page 80).

WAYS OF GROWING BULBS

Bulbs can be grown in a number of different ways: in clay or plastic containers, either singly in the case of the large-growing hippeastrum, or together to form an arrangement of plants flowering at the same time. If you are making an arrangement to include the smaller bulbs that prefer to remain in cool conditions, it is best to grow them separately and then carefully transplant them into the container once they are in bud. Use a well-drained, peat-based compost or special bulb fibre. The latter has the advantage of being cleaner to use than ordinary soil and is more successful if you are using pots without drainage holes.

Crocus, hyacinth and the Tazetta narcissi will flower and look most attractive in a simple shallow bowl filled with pebbles and enough water to cover the roots. The bulbs can be wedged in among the pebbles, and obviously must not be allowed to dry out. Crocus and hyacinth will also grow in plain water in a bulb glass. This consists of a jar with a cup-like top, on which the bulb rests. A piece of charcoal added to the water will keep it sweet. The base of the bulb should be just clear of the water – the roots will bridge the gap, and will coil right down into the jar. Children especially find this a fascinating method of growing bulbs.

Another container designed for bulbs is a

clay pot with holes in the sides. Crocus bulbs grow out through these, as well as on the top in the normal manner, and make a more impressive display than they would do in a standard pot.

Only those bulbs which have been grown in compost will be worth saving for flowering outside in following years. Bulbs grown in bulb fibre may take rather longer to recover than those grown in soil. Bulbs grown in water, however, must be discarded since they will have exhausted their resources.

Growing and forcing hardy bulbs Place a layer of peat-based compost or moistened bulb fibre in the bottom of the container, put in the bulbs and fill in between with compost. The necks of larger bulbs like narcissus and hyacinth should be left exposed, but smaller bulbs should be covered over. The soil level should be below the rim of the pot. Moisten, but do not soak, the compost, cover the pots with black polythene and either sink them up to their rims in soil outside or keep them in the coolest spot available in the house – the best temperature is about 4°C (40°F) – and leave them for 8-10 weeks. This process is essential for the plants to develop their roots. Tulips, being later-flowering, need a longer period of up to 16 weeks.

At the end of this period the pot will be full of roots and there should be shoots about 2·5cm (1in) high. Bring them in to slightly warmer conditions, 10°C (50°F) being ideal. It is at this stage that the flowering stems and leaves develop and much higher temperatures will accelerate the process, encouraging leaf growth at the expense of bud development.

When the buds have formed, the plants can be brought in to warmer conditions. Most of these hardy bulbs will fare better and last longer in a temperature of about 16°C (60°F). Keep them moist.

If you want to have bulbs in flower in time for Christmas, it is best to buy the ones which have been commercially prepared. Pot these up in the autumn and keep them cool as described above, then bring them into warmer conditions in the middle of November.

Bulb glasses make a feature of roots as well as flowers

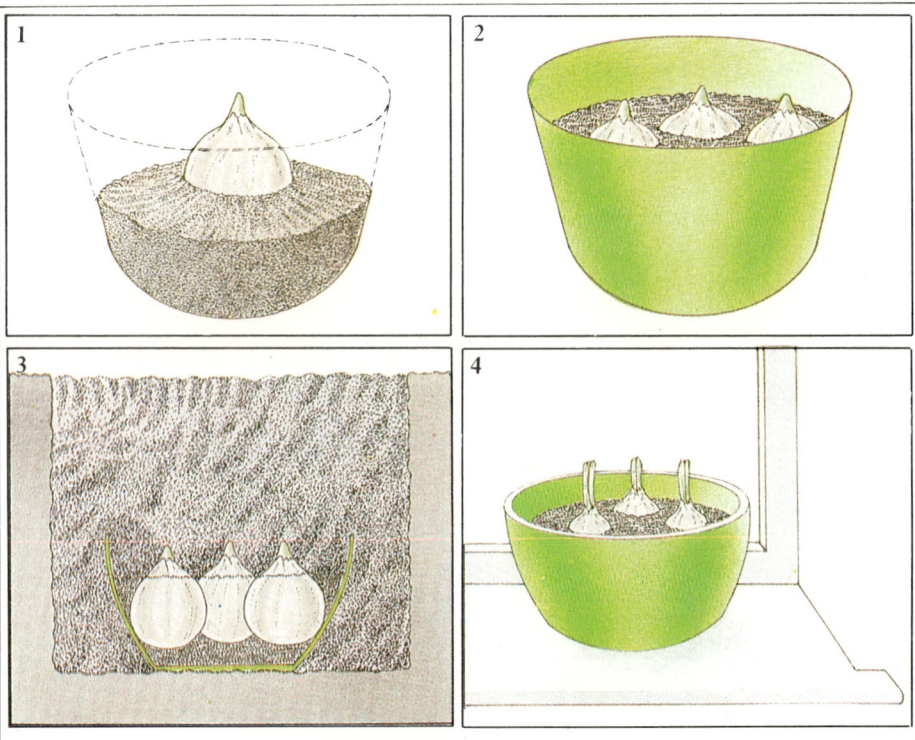

Preparing bulbs for growing indoors: 1 set bulbs in a layer of fibre; 2 firm down more fibre around them, leaving the necks of larger bulbs showing; 3 sink in ashes or cover with black polythene, and keep cool for 8-16 weeks; 4 bring them into their flowering positions

Magnificent displays of pot-grown bulbs: clockwise from top left these are Easter lily (Lilium longiflorum); tulips and hyacinths in a wooden tub; hyacinths, very fragrant, and with a festive touch; crocuses; snowdrops (Galanthus nivalis); and finally the popular daffodil King Alfred

A-Z OF HOUSEPLANTS

On the following pages many of the best flowering and foliage houseplants are described, and their needs and fads are listed. For success with houseplants consult this A – Z before you buy, to make sure of acquiring only those species which will thrive in the conditions you can offer them. Buying a plant before you know what it wants is more risky – but can still be great fun.

ABUTILON STRIATUM THOMPSONII

Abutilon – flower

ACHIMENES

**Guatemala
Hot water plant
22-30cm (9-12in)**

ABUTILON STRIATUM THOMPSONII

**Brazil
Flowering maple
To 1·2m (4ft)**

This graceful and unusual, tall-growing, summer-flowering plant is worth growing for its fine, maple-shaped, green and yellow, mottled leaves, which hang from arching stems. Bell-shaped orange flowers with crimson veins are freely borne, either singly or in clusters, from spring to autumn.

Conditions A bright and well-lit position is essential, with shading from very bright sun. Provide average temperatures, between 10 and 15°C (50-60°F). In heated rooms give some ventilation, and if possible allow periods outside during the summer. Abutilon needs to be supported with canes.

Care Water freely from spring through to autumn, and keep almost dry in winter when the plant is resting. Mist the leaves occasionally in summer. Give fortnightly liquid feeds in the growing season.

Pruning/trimming Trim back side shoots in spring, and cut the plant back to half its size in autumn, to promote strong bushy growth and prevent legginess.

Potting on Pot on annually in spring, if the roots have filled the pot, in a loam-based compost (John Innes No. 2). Place broken crocks in the base of the pot to aid drainage.

Propagation Take half-ripe cuttings in spring, or grow from seed.

Problems May be prone to attack by mealy bug.

A free-flowering plant growing from a rhizome; it dies back in the autumn and can be restarted in the spring. Tubular flowers cover the plant from summer to late autumn, and are brightly coloured in a range of pinks and mauves to dark reds and purples. The leaves are bright mid-green and hairy, and its trailing stems make this a suitable plant for growing in a hanging basket or container. For a more upright and bushy pot plant, regularly pinch out the tips of young side shoots; it may also be necessary to provide some form of support.

Conditions Achimenes needs a warm, well-lit position shaded from direct sun, with a minimum temperature of 13°C (55°F) during the growing season. Keep the pot plunged in a container of moist peat or moss to provide some humidity.

Care Keep the compost moist at all times during flowering. Mist occasionally around the plant, but avoid wetting the hairy leaf surfaces. Give a monthly liquid feed from bud-formation until the flowers begin to die back.

After flowering Stop watering altogether and allow the stems to die back naturally before cutting them back. Allow the rhizomes to dry out completely, then either store them in their pots, or in dry peat or sand at a winter temperature of no less than 13°C (55°F). In March, take out carefully and separate the rhizomes, which may each have produced up to six new growths during the previous season. They are brittle and must be handled carefully. Pot up in a soil-less compost with small quantities of loam and sharp sand added, or in John Innes No. 2 potting compost, six tubers to each 15cm (6in) pot. To start the plant up in spring, immerse the whole pot in warm water, and thereafter water sparingly until signs of vigorous growth appear.

Propagation By division of the rhizomes in March as explained above; from seed in spring; or cuttings from new shoots in May.

Problems Give an occasional misting of water if there are signs of red spider mite (a symptom of dry air); otherwise generally trouble-free.

ADIANTUM CAPILLUS-VENERIS

**Subtropical and temperate zones
Maidenhair fern
To 23cm (9in)**

Dark wiry stems carry light green fronds of small filmy leaflets in an upright and arching shape. A lovely, though fragile plant, it needs careful handling and the right conditions to thrive and look its best.

Conditions Give a position in indirect light, such as a north- or east-facing windowsill. Avoid draughts and contact with heat and gas fumes. A temperature of between 16 and 21°C (60-70°F) is best, with a minimum winter temperature of 13°C (55°F). It needs a high degree of humidity in the atmosphere, and in heated rooms pots can be kept in larger containers of moist peat, or standing in a shallow bowl or tray of damp gravel or pebbles; but never allow the plant to stand in water.

Care Compost should be kept moist at all times but never allowed to become water-

ADIANTUM

logged, as this results in root rot. Reduce watering during winter. In dry-heat conditions, mist around the plant, but avoid damaging the delicate fronds with too much water. Give fortnightly liquid feeds during the growing season.

Potting on Repot annually in spring, if the roots have filled the pot, using a soil-less compost, with coarse sand for drainage. Be careful not to bury the crown of the plant.

Propagation Divide well-grown plants in spring, or raise new plants from spores taken from the underside of mature fronds. Successful propagation from spores requires a high level of humidity – a heated propagator is really essential.

Problems These usually arise from incorrect treatment – in particular from failure to provide the right conditions. Brown tips and yellowing, falling fronds usually indicate that the air is too hot and dry. Limpness is likely to be the result of incorrect watering – either too much or too little. Pale fronds with scorch marks indicate exposure to sun; the plant should be moved to a shadier spot. Weak growth may be the result of unsuitable conditions or insufficient feeding.

ACHIMENES

AECHMEA FASCIATA

Brazil
Urn plant
To 60cm (2ft)

One of the most popular and commonly seen of the flowering bromeliads, *A. fasciata* is a large, dramatic-looking plant with stiff, silvery, grey-green banded leaves. These are covered with a whitish, floury substance which rubs off easily, and they form a central vase or urn, from which the spike of the flower head emerges. This urn gives the plant its common name. The small lavender-coloured flowers are themselves fairly short-lived and insignificant; it is the colourful pink bracts that form the main feature of the plant, and these may appear at any time of the year and last for up to four months. As with all bromeliads,

the parent plant begins to die off as flowering begins, so propagation is necessary; the parent rosette may remain attractive for some considerable time even though it is technically dying.

Conditions Give a brightly lit, warm position, out of direct sun but with a temperature of at least 21°C (70°F) to encourage it to flower. Once flowering has started, a lower temperature of about 16°C (60°F) will keep it in flower longer. Mist the leaves regularly.

Care While it is growing and flowering, aechmea needs to be watered in two separate ways. Pour water into the central vase of the plant, and keep this filled up, using rainwater or tepid soft water. Empty and refill the vase every 2-3 months. The compost itself should be kept no more than

moist, and never allowed to become waterlogged. After flowering and in winter, keep the rosette and compost barely moist. Give a weak liquid feed once a month, either added to the water in the vase, or in the form of a foliar spray.

Potting on This is rarely necessary since plants do best in small pots – 20cm (7in) for the largest plants. The general rule is not to pot on until the rosette can no longer be accommodated by the pot.

Propagation By offsets that appear after flowering; cut away the parent rosette as it begins to rot, and pot up the offsets. See the general section on *Bromeliads*, page 17.

Problems Brown tips on the leaves may be due to insufficient water in the vase of the plant, lack of humidity in the atmosphere, or to the use of hard water. Overwatering of the compost may cause rotting – keep moist, but never wet. Scale and mealy bug may attack.

AGAVE VICTORIAE REGINAE

Mexico
15cm (6in)

The agaves are a wide group of rosette-forming succulents with sword-shaped leaves. *A. victoriae reginae* has fleshy, dark green leaves marked with fine white lines and tapering to a spine at the tip. The tightly packed rosette sits on the soil surface and will spread gradually to a circumference of 50cm (20in) over a long period of time. Plants do not flower until they reach maturity, which may be after 50 years or more. A long flowering stem rises from the centre of the plant; flowering is followed by death of the rosette. More commonly seen, but less suitable for small spaces, is *A. americana* 'Marginata', which has long sword-shaped leaves, variegated green and yellow, and which can reach a length of 1·2m (4ft) or more.

Conditions Grow in a well-lit position, such as a sunny windowsill. Temperature

AECHMEA FASCIATA

AGAVE VICTORIAE REGINAE

should be warm in summer and cooler in winter, with a minimum of 10°C (50°F). Allow good ventilation or stand outside in sunny weather.

Care Agaves need more moisture than most other succulents in the growing period. Water well in summer, very sparingly in winter. A layer of fine gravel on the surface of the soil will prevent water from accumulating around the plant and causing the base to rot.

Potting on Repot when necessary in spring, using a well-balanced rich mixture, such as John Innes No. 2 potting compost. Put a layer of broken crocks in the base of the pot to ensure good drainage.

Propagation From seed sown in April and germinated at a temperature of 21°C (70°F).

Problems Rotting at the base and wilting of the leaves indicate overwatering or poor drainage. Hard dry brown spots on the leaves may be caused by insufficient water in the growing season.

See also the section on *Cacti and Succulents*, page 21-22.

AGLAONEMA 'SILVER QUEEN'

Philippines
Chinese evergreen
30-60cm (1-2ft)

A foliage plant with large, lance-shaped leaves, variegated green and silver. Some mature plants may produce arum-like flower spathes. Its tolerance of shade makes aglaonema a good plant for problem corners.

Conditions Needs a shaded spot away from direct sun and will grow in a dark position. Aglaonema needs a constant temperature, ideally between 16 and 21°C (60-70°F) all year round. Winter temperatures should never drop below 13°C (55°F), and avoid draughts and exposure to gas fumes. A high degree of humidity is required, so keep the pot in a container of moist peat, and mist the leaves regularly.

Care Water thoroughly during the growing season, and sparingly in winter. Give occasional weak liquid feeds from spring to autumn.

Potting on Pot on in spring when the plant appears pot-bound, usually every three years. Use a well-drained soil-less compost or John Innes No. 2 or 3.

Propagation From small suckers at the base of the stem. Detach with a few leaves and roots and pot on in April.

Problems Shrivelled leaves and brown tips and edges usually indicate low temperatures, dryness or exposure to draughts. Infestation by mealy bug amongst the leaf stalks can be a problem. Red spider will attack if conditions are too dry.

AGLAONEMA 'SILVER QUEEN'

ALOE VARIEGATA

APHELANDRA SQUARROSA 'LOUISAE'

ALOE VARIEGATA

Cape Province
Partridge-breasted aloe
To 30cm (1ft)

A large family of rosette-forming succulents which vary widely in size. *A. variegata* is the species most commonly seen, with overlapping pointed leaves of dark green, banded white, which form a small rosette about 10cm (4in) wide. In spring orange flowers appear on a tall spike above the rosette.

Conditions Provide a position in full light, preferably a sunny windowsill, and allow good ventilation in summer. Give warmth in summer and cooler conditions in winter, with a minimum of 5°C (41°F). No humidity is required.

Care Water well in summer, and drain thoroughly. Water sparingly in winter, particularly if plants are kept cool; a well-tended plant should have plenty of water stored away in its leaves from the summer months. Give an occasional weak liquid feed between April and September.

Potting on In spring when necessary, using a well-drained compost such as a mixture of loam, peat and coarse sand, or John Innes No. 2 with some added sand. Keep plants in shallow pots.

Propagation In summer from small offsets at the base of the plant, which are detached and allowed to dry for a couple of days before being potted up individually.

Problems Most likely to be caused by incorrect watering. Wilting is the result of inadequate water in summer. Yellowing leaves accompanied by rotting at the base is the result of overwatering plants kept in cool winter conditions. A properly watered plant can resist most pests and diseases, although mealy bugs may attack.

See also the general section on *Cacti and Succulents*, pages 21-22.

APHELANDRA SQUARROSA 'LOUISAE'

Brazil
Zebra plant
22-45cm (9-18in)

A popular plant with interesting evergreen foliage and bold, brilliant yellow bracts, freely borne from July to September. The slightly drooping leaves are up to 22cm (9in) long and are a dark shining green with bold ivory lines along their main veins. Small yellow tubular flowers emerge from the sides of the cone-shaped column of bracts and last for up to three weeks. After flowering the bracts turn green. *A. s.* 'Brockfeld' is a smaller cultivar with larger, more upright leaves and stronger markings.

Conditions Grow in a draught-free spot, brightly lit but away from direct sun. Keep warm, with a minimum winter temperature of 14·5°C (58°F). Provide a humid atmosphere by placing the pot on moist pebbles or in damp peat.

Care Keep compost moist at all times with tepid soft water, but never allow it to become waterlogged. Reduce watering in the winter months. Mist around leaves daily from spring to autumn. Aphelandra needs constant year-round feeding, once a week in summer and fortnightly during the rest of the year. Remove flower heads when they begin to rot, which will be after the bracts have turned green.

Pruning When the bracts have died back, reduce growth to three-quarters of its original height, back to a strong pair of leaves.

Potting on Repot in spring when necessary, using John Innes No. 2 potting compost. Water sparingly for the first few weeks after repotting.

Propagation Take 7·5-10cm (3-4in) cuttings from side shoots at pruning time, or from the new side shoots that develop afterwards. Root in equal quantities of sand and peat in a propagator, and pot on into 7·5cm (3in) pots when established.

Problems Loss of leaves is usually a symptom of inadequate watering, but could also be caused by low temperatures, too much sun or exposure to draughts. Brown tips on leaves are caused by insufficient humidity – plunge the pot in moist peat, and mist frequently. The leaves of 'Louisae' have a natural tendency to droop slightly, but will wilt dramatically if the compost dries out.

ARAUCARIA EXCELSA

New Zealand Norfolk Island pine
To 1·5m (5ft)

A conifer, related to the monkey puzzle tree. Tiered branches radiate from the central stem in a pyramidal shape, with feathery looking needles in shades of pale to dark green. It is best grown alone in a spot where the branches have plenty of growing space.

Conditions Keep in a brightly lit or semi-shaded position, out of direct sun, and turn the plant regularly to encourage symmetrical growth. Maintain a moderate to cool temperature, with a minimum of 7°C (45°F) in winter. Keep the needles misted if the atmosphere is dry, and give some ventilation in summer or stand outside from June to August.

Care Keep the compost moist and ensure adequate drainage; never allow the plant to become wet or waterlogged. Water sparingly in the winter. Give occasional liquid feeds during the growing season. Do not trim or prune.

Potting on Top-dress in spring, or pot on if necessary. Since the shape of the plant deteriorates over a height of 1·5m (5ft), it is best kept pot-bound to restrict growth. Grow in a well-drained loam-based potting medium such as John Innes No. 2.

Propagation From seed sown in spring.

Problems Usually the result of incorrect treatment. Falling needles may indicate waterlogging, an atmosphere that is too dry, or exposure to sun. Otherwise the plant is generally trouble-free.

ARAUCARIA EXCELSA

ASPARAGUS SPRENGERI

ASPARAGUS PLUMOSUS

ASPARAGUS

South Africa
Asparagus fern

Despite their appearance these are not true ferns, but members of the lily family. They are fast growers, and less exacting in their requirements than the true ferns. Mature plants may bear small clusters of insignificant green-white flowers in June and July, sometimes followed by berries.

A. plumosus will grow to 1m (3ft) in height with an upright habit and horizontal branches on fine stems, and tiny, dark green, feathery, needle-like leaves. In time it will develop into a climber.

A. sprengeri has longer arching stems growing to 60-90cm (2-3ft) long with coarser, bright green, prickly 'needles'. Its form makes it very suitable for hanging baskets or for a position where it can cascade over the pot.

Conditions Asparagus ferns are adaptable to a variety of conditions, growing in bright light or semi-shade, but out of direct sun. They need moderate temperatures, not less than 7°C (45°F) in winter.

Care Water regularly from spring to summer and keep compost just moist in winter. In a hot dry atmosphere mist occasionally. Give occasional liquid feeds over the growing period. Trim back occasionally to encourage bushy growth and prevent a leggy appearance, particularly in the case of *A. sprengeri*.

Potting on Examine the root ball annually in spring, and if necessary repot in John Innes No. 2 potting compost with added sand for drainage.

Propagation By division at almost any time of year. Make sure the compost is moist before dividing.

Problems Usually the result of incorrect treatment. Yellowing and falling leaves usually indicate conditions that are too hot and dry. Overwatering the plant or allowing it to stand with the roots in water may cause root rot.

ASPIDISTRA ELATIOR

China
Cast iron plant
To 50cm (20in)

A member of the lily family, aspidistra was a favourite Victorian houseplant and is now regaining favour. It is a handsome, large-leaved foliage plant, well known for its robust constitution, which is reflected in the common name. It will tolerate poor light, draughts and general neglect, though it obviously responds gratefully to more favourable treatment. Long, lance-shaped, glossy, dark green leaves grow directly from a number of short stalks. Occasionally, small purple flowers appear at the base of the plant. 'Variegata' has cream and green striped leaves, and is only a little more demanding than the type.

Conditions Aspidistra prefers a shady position out of the sun, and will grow in quite dark corners. Although it will tolerate a wide range of temperatures, average to cool conditions are best, with a minimum of 7°C (45°F) in winter.

Care Water enough to keep compost moist in the growing season, sparingly in winter, and avoid overwatering at all times. Sponge the leaves with plain tepid water occasionally, but do not use leaf-shine or other proprietary foliar cleaners. Give monthly liquid feeds during the growing season.

Potting on Since it is a slow-growing plant and tends to do best when pot-bound, pot on only every four or five years in spring, using a loam-based compost.

Propagation This is by division in spring or summer, preferably when potting on.

Problems Generally trouble-free, provided the plant is kept out of the sun and is not allowed to become waterlogged. Avoid getting chemicals on the foliage.

ASPLENIUM

Tropical Asia, Pacific Islands
Bird's nest fern, spleenwort
30-60cm (12-24in)

Asplenium nidus has large, glossy, spear-shaped fronds growing up and out from a central rosette; they are bright green with dark central ribs and wavy margins.

The finely divided, mid-green fronds of *A. bulbiferum* bush out from wiry stems. The mature fronds produce plantlets or 'bulbils' on their upper surfaces, and new plants grow from these.

Conditions Grow in a shaded position, out of sun and away from draughts and direct contact with heat. A temperature between

ASPLENIUM NIDUS

16 and 21°C (60-70°F) is ideal, with a minimum of 10°C (50°F) for *A. bulbiferum* and 13°C (55°F) for *A. nidus*. Provide humidity by keeping pots in a container filled either with damp peat or sphagnum moss.

Care Keep compost moist at all times, but never allow plants to stand in water or become waterlogged. Water more sparingly in cool winter conditions. Mist regularly, and keep the leaves of *A. nidus* clean by sponging with water occasionally.

Potting on Inspect the root ball annually in spring and repot if necessary, using a soil-less compost with added coarse sand for drainage. *A. nidus*, in particular, demands a high proportion of fibrous peat. Take care not to bury the crown of the plant when replanting.

Propagation *A. nidus* from spores sown in a propagator in March, July or August; *A. bulbiferum* from leaflets bearing bulbils, placed on a moist, peat-based compost. Pot on separately when roots are established.

Problems Generally trouble-free, provided plants are not overwatered or exposed to hot dry conditions.

ASPIDISTRA ELATIOR

AZALEA INDICA

AZALEA INDICA

India
Azalea
60cm (2ft)

This is the type usually sold as a flowering pot plant in late winter and early spring. It has small, neat, evergreen leaves and clusters of single or double, brightly coloured flowers in shades of white, pink, orange and red. Choose a plant which has plenty of buds showing colour, and one or two open flowers.

Conditions The three imperatives are a position in bright light, shaded from direct sun; a temperature on the cool side, preferably between 10 and 16°C (50-60°F); and copious watering.

Care during flowering Thorough and frequent watering is essential to keep the plant healthy and in flower for the longest possible time. The compost should be kept moist continually, and there should be a water mark about 1·25cm (½in) from the base of the stem. Lower means it is dry, higher that it is waterlogged. Use rainwater whenever possible, otherwise tepid, preferably soft, tap water. Water by the immersion method (see page 116) two or three times a week, but do not allow the plant to remain standing in water. Stand pots in containers filled with moist peat or in damp gravel trays. Do not feed during flowering.

Care after flowering When flowering has finished, place in a shady spot outside or a cool spot inside. Water regularly, and feed fortnightly with a fertilizer for acid-loving plants. Mist the leaves if they look dry, and when new buds form, top-dress with peat or repot in peaty compost. Cut back any dead wood and move inside or into the flowering position.

Problems These are invariably related to incorrect treatment. Shrivelled and falling leaves indicate underwatering or an atmosphere which is too hot and dry. Yellowing of the leaves (chlorosis) is probably the result of lime in the water: use rainwater whenever possible, or treat with sequestrene.

BEGONIA × LUCERNA

Brazil
Spotted angel's wing begonia
To 1·8m (6ft)

This is one of the fibrous-rooted begonias with tall cane stems. The leaves are large, olive-green, splashed with silver and flushed red on the undersides. Pink flowers are borne freely on large pendent clusters all through the spring and summer. *B. haagiana*, the elephant's ear begonia, is a bushier plant, growing to 1.2m (4ft) with large, hairy, prominently veined leaves.

BEGONIA × LUCERNA

Conditions Place in a well-lit position out of direct sun. Temperatures should be moderate to warm, with a minimum of 13°C (55°F); *B. haagiana* will tolerate 7°C (45°F). Give some humidity by standing pots on wet gravel or sinking them in moist peat. Mist around plants, and take care not to expose them to gas fumes.

Care As for *Begonia rex*.

Potting on In spring, when necessary, in a peat-based compost.

Propagation From stem cuttings between May and August.

Problems As for *B. rex*.

BEGONIA REX

Assam
30cm (1ft)

A decorative foliage plant with large heart-shaped leaves in a wide variety of dramatic patterns and colours, ranging from palest pinks and greens to deep reds and purple-blacks. *B. masoniana*, the iron cross begonia, has a grey-green leaf with a distinctive dark cross in the centre. It tends to be a short-lived plant and under ordinary house conditions may not last longer than one or two years.

Conditions Give a well-lit position out of direct contact with the sun. *B. rex* does best in an average temperature of about 18°C (65°F), with a minimum winter temperature of 13°C (55°F). Avoid hot dry conditions and give moisture in the surrounding atmosphere by standing the plant on a shallow tray of damp gravel. Do not mist or wet the leaves directly. Avoid exposure to gas fumes.

Care Water regularly in the growing season, but allow the compost to become almost dry in between waterings. Keep barely moist in the dormant period. Give occasional liquid feeds from spring to autumn.

Potting on Examine the root ball annually in spring and pot on when necessary. Use wide shallow pots filled with a well-drained peat-based compost.

Propagation Propagate by division of rhizomes at potting time, using a section of the rhizome with some roots attached; alternatively take leaf cuttings in summer, pinning the leaves down to the compost with the veins cut (see notes on *Propagation*, page 125-6).

Problems Mildew, which appears as white patches on leaves, is a result of cold, dark, damp and airless conditions.

BEGONIA REX

BEGONIA SEMPERFLORENS

BEGONIA TUBERHYBRIDA

BEGONIA SEMPERFLORENS

Brazil
15-22·5cm (6-9in)

These fibrous-rooted begonias have a neat bushy growth habit. They are often grown as summer bedding plants, but are equally successful indoors. The small rounded leaves are glossy green or purple-red, and masses of small, white or pink flowers are borne throughout the summer – longer in the right conditions.

Conditions Grow in bright light but give some shade from hot sun. Temperatures should be moderate to warm, with a minimum of 10°C (50°F) in winter. Provide as much light as possible during the winter months to encourage flowering and good foliage colour. Mist regularly, and provide some ventilation in summer. Give monthly feeds if plants are kept for a second year.

Care Keep well watered during flowering; see *B. rex.*

Potting on If keeping for a second year, repot in spring in a well-drained compost.

Propagation Grow from seed sown in March or April for plants ready to flower from October onwards.

Problems Generally trouble-free.

BEGONIA TUBERHYBRIDA

South America
60cm (2ft)

The tuberous group of begonias consists of temporary houseplants making spectacular displays for the summer and autumn. The grandiflora group includes the largest-flowering tuberous begonias, which carry double flowers up to 15cm (6in) or more in diameter, in shades of yellow, orange, pink, scarlet or white. Some have frilled edges or petals margined in a contrasting colour.

The multifloras produce a large number of small single flowers; the multiflora maxima types have large sprays of double blooms. Both are more compact in habit than the grandifloras and are better where space is restricted. Use canes to support the stems.

Conditions Grow the plants in a good light but avoid direct sun. Give moderate temperatures – not less than 13°C (55°F). Provide humidity by surrounding the pots with damp peat, and mist the compost frequently.

Care during flowering Keep the soil moist but allow to dry slightly in between waterings. Blooms will be encouraged to grow larger if all female flower heads are removed (these are easily recognized by the seed capsule behind the petals). Give a liquid feed every two weeks from when the flower buds are forming until the end of the flowering period.

Care after flowering Gradually withhold water as the stems turn yellow. When the leaves have died down, twist the stems off and place the tubers in a cool dry place in sand, which should occasionally be sprinkled with tepid water. Repot the tubers in spring in 7·5cm (3in) pots with the hollow side of the tuber uppermost, and in a temperature of about 18°C (65°F). Keep the soil barely moist until new shoots appear, and as the plant develops, pot on into a mixture of 2 parts leaf mould and 1 part sand.

Propagation In April, cut tubers into sections, making sure each section has at least one shoot. Pot in equal parts of peat and sand. Alternatively take stem cuttings with a heel.

Problems Pale, rotting leaves are likely to be caused by overwatering. Yellow leaves are a result of either too much or too little water. Leaf loss may be caused by lack of light if stems are thin and leggy, too much heat if leaves are dry, or too much water if leaves are wilted and rotten. Loss of buds and leaves turning brown at the tips are usually caused by lack of humidity. Check regularly for aphid and red spider mite.

BELOPERONE GUTTATA

BELOPERONE GUTTATA

Mexico
Shrimp plant
45-60cm (1½-2ft)

A small twiggy plant with pointed, oval, soft green leaves. Small pendent shrimp-like flower heads, white with overlapping salmon-coloured bracts, are borne almost continuously from April to December.

Conditions Grow in a bright position with shade from hot sun. Average to cool conditions, with a minimum of 7°C (45°F) in winter, will keep the plant in flower longer.

Care Water frequently and thoroughly during the growing and flowering season and keep the pot on a pebble tray if conditions are hot and dry, but do not allow it to stand in water or become waterlogged.

Reduce watering in winter. Mist occasionally. Give weekly liquid feeds from April to September.

Pruning Plants can be cut back as much as half after flowering to encourage bushy growth, and pinching out shoots from time to time will have the same effect. Remove the flowering bracts of young plants for the first few months to promote sturdier, better-flowering growth.

Potting on Examine the root ball annually, and when necessary pot on into a well-drained loam-based compost such as John Innes No. 2 with added peat, or a soil-less compost.

Propagation From stem cuttings taken when trimming the plant.

Problems Generally trouble-free.

BILLBERGIA NUTANS

BILLBERGIA NUTANS

South America
Queen's tears
To 45cm (1½ft)

One of the most easily grown bromeliads (see also pages 15-18), *Billbergia nutans* has narrow, dark green, grass-like leaves and clusters of small green and purple flowers hanging from pendulous pink bracts. *B. windii* has grey-green leaves, pale green flowers and rose-pink bracts on long arching stems, but is a more difficult plant to grow.

Conditions Grow billbergias in a position of bright light but shaded from direct sun. Give moderate temperatures, minimum 7-10°C (45-50°F) in winter, although *B. nutans* will tolerate cooler conditions. Mist the leaves regularly if the atmosphere is hot and dry.

Care Keep the vase filled with tepid water, and the compost moist but not waterlogged during the growing and flowering season. Reduce watering in winter so that the vase and soil are barely moist. Use rainwater or tepid soft water whenever possible. Give occasional weak liquid feeds during the summer months.

Potting on Repot when the rosette can no longer be accommodated by the pot, using a well-drained peat-based compost.

Propagation From well-grown offsets after flowering is over.

Problems These usually arise from incorrect treatment. Brown tips on the leaves may be due to insufficient water in the vase, or to the atmosphere being too dry, or to the use of hard water. Avoid overwatering the compost.

CALADIUM 'CANDIDUM'

Tropical South America
Angel's wings
30-45cm (1-1½ft)

A tuberous plant best treated as a flowering houseplant, since the foliage dies down in late summer or early autumn. All caladiums make beautiful and striking specimen plants with huge, papery, arrow-shaped leaves, 30cm (1ft) or more in length. *C.* 'Candidum' has white leaves with delicate tracery markings in green. Other caladium hybrids have leaves with markings in vivid reds, greens and creams. 'Candidum' is the most readily available and the easiest of a delicate group.

Conditions Give the plants a position in good light with shading from direct sun. A constant warm temperature of around 21°C (70°F) is best, and never lower than 16°C (60°F). A high degree of humidity is required, and plants are best grown among other plants needing similar conditions. Give protection from draughts.

Care when in leaf Water generously and frequently and drain thoroughly from spring

CALADIUM 'CANDIDUM'

until the leaves begin to wither in early autumn. Give weekly liquid feeds. As the leaves begin to fade, reduce watering and stop feeding.

Care after leaf die-back Allow the soil to dry out completely and store the tubers at a temperature of about 13°C (55°F) in a rich humus potting compost. In spring, bring into a temperature of 21°C (70°F) and keep compost moist until shoots appear. Keep well watered and begin weekly feeds.

Propagation Small offsets, detached from the tubers when repotting in March, and potted up in the same way, should produce good-sized tubers in one to two years.

Problems Any problem (such as premature withering of the leaves) is likely to be caused by failure to provide suitable conditions: constant warmth and a high degree of humidity are essential.

CALATHEA MAKOYANA

Brazil
Peacock plant
To 60cm (2ft)

These striking foliage plants are closely related to the Maranta family, and are sometimes sold under that name. *C. makoyana* has paper-fine, rounded oblong leaves, silvery-green in colour with irregular dark green blotches on the veins above and maroon blotches beneath.

Conditions Grow in a light position shaded from direct sun to protect the colour of the leaves. The plant needs constant warmth, with a winter minimum temperature of 13-16°C (55-60°F). A high degree of humidity is needed, and pots are best kept plunged in containers of moist peat or sphagnum moss. Bottle gardens give ideal conditions.

Care During the growing season keep the compost constantly moist, using tepid soft water – rainwater when possible. Reduce watering in winter. Give liquid feeds once a week from spring to autumn.

Potting on When roots fill the container (normally annually) repot in June and July. Use a peat-based compost with good drainage, or John Innes No. 2 potting compost.

Propagation By division at repotting time. Keep warm and moist, preferably in a propagator, until established.

Problems Most problems are likely to be due to underwatering and an inadequate degree of humidity – and this in turn may give rise to infestation by red spider mite. Discoloured leaves indicate exposure to sun. White deposits on the leaves are probably due to the use of hard tap water instead of rainwater.

CALATHEA MAKOYANA

Calceolaria

South America
Slipper plant
20-30cm (8-12in)

Temporary flowering houseplants with curious, pouch-shaped blooms in shades of orange and yellow and covered with crimson/brown blotches. Purchased when in bloom in early spring they will normally continue to flower for about a month, and should be discarded when flowering is over.

Conditions Grow in a well-ventilated room in bright indirect light. Cool temperatures of below 16°C (60°F) are ideal. The plants will wilt in warm positions with direct sun.

Care Keep compost moist at all times, but avoid waterlogging. Because the flower is easily stained, it is better to water the plant from beneath, using rainwater whenever possible. Mist around the plant occasionally, and avoid draughts.

Propagation From seed sown during the previous summer, but this is a specialist task.

Problems Check the plants regularly for infestation by aphids.

Capsicum annuum

Tropics
Christmas pepper
45cm (1½ft)

These decorative plants are usually treated as annuals, and grown for their brightly coloured fruits which can last for two or three months in the right conditions. The peppers emerge in the late summer after flowering time, and may be round, oblong or conical, sometimes twisted, and coloured yellow, orange or red. Plants bought when the fruit is still green will last longer.

Conditions Keep in a bright airy position with some sun. Temperature should be cool, but not less than 13°C (55°F) in win-

CALCEOLARIA

CAPSICUM ANNUUM

ter. Give some humidity by keeping pots plunged in containers of moist peat, and misting regularly; hot dry conditions will cause premature fruit fall.

Care Water moderately; occasionally immerse pots to the rim in a bowl of tepid water, then allow to drain thoroughly before returning to the saucer. Mist daily when plants are in flower to encourage fruit setting, and give a weak liquid feed at ten day intervals from the time the fruits appear until they begin to show colour. Discard plants when the fruit has dropped.

Propagation From seed sown in spring, at temperatures between 15 and 18°C (60-65°F). Pot up seedlings individually in a loam-based compost.

Problems Yellowing and falling leaves and fruits are the result of either high temperatures and/or of overwatering. In these conditions plants are also susceptible to red spider mite.

CELOSIA PLUMOSA PYRAMIDALIS

**South-east Asia
To 60cm (2ft)**

Decorative flowering annuals which are usually grown as outdoor bedding plants, but do equally well as indoor pot plants. Tall feathery plumes rise above the leaves from July to September and, according to strain, may be yellow, orange or red. The flowers of some strains can be dried and used for winter decoration.

Conditions Place in a well-ventilated and bright spot, with shading from direct sun. Keep cool, at a temperature of 10-16°C (50-60°F).

Care Water well when the compost feels dry on the surface, and do not rewater until it begins to dry out again. Celosias which are kept permanently moist may rot, or wilt and never recover. Discard plants when flowering is over, keeping a few flower heads for winter arrangements.

Propagation From seed sown in spring. Give seedlings good light as soon as they start to produce true leaves, and pot on when the roots have filled the pot.

Problems Generally related to incorrect care – temperatures which are too high and overwatering are the most common causes of failure.

CELOSIA PLUMOSA PYRAMIDALIS

Ceropegia woodii

Natal
Hearts entangled, rosary vine
To 1m (3ft)

A strange but charming trailing succulent which grows from a tuber. The dainty heart-shaped leaves are fleshy, and are marbled green and silver with purple undersides. They grow in well-spaced pairs on long, thread-like stems. Clusters of small, pinky-purple flowers appear in autumn and can last for up to six weeks.

Conditions Grow in a position of indirect light or semi-shade. Temperatures should be warm in summer, and slightly cooler in winter – 10°C (50°F) – though higher winter temperatures will be tolerated.

Care In summer allow the soil almost to dry out before watering well and draining thoroughly. In winter water very sparingly: enough to prevent the leaves from shrivel-ling. Overwatering may rot the tuber. Give occasional very weak liquid feeds with a standard houseplant fertilizer during spring and summer.

Potting on Repot in spring when plants become too crowded or when the pot is full of roots. Use a rich, loam-based soil with added humus.

Propagation From small tubers which sometimes form at the leaf joints. Detach these with a portion of the stem and pot up, using the normal potting mixture with some added sand.

Problems Generally trouble-free, but yellowing leaves may indicate rotting of the tuber, due either to overwatering or to winter temperatures that are too low. Remove soil from around the tuber and allow it to dry out if the damage is not too severe. Unfortunately, if the tuber has rotted the condition cannot be reversed, and the plant will have to be discarded.

CEROPEGIA WOODII

Chamaedorea elegans
(Syn. Neanthe bella)

Mexico
Parlour palm
To 1·2m (4ft)

One of the smallest and easiest of the palms, chamaedorea is an upright plant with stiffly arching, dark grey-green fronds. Small green flowers may appear on even very young plants, and though they do not add greatly to the appearance, the seed may be saved for propagation.

Conditions Grow in a shaded position away from direct sun. The plants need moderate to warm temperatures in summer, and cooler in winter with a minimum of 10°C (50°F). Provide some humidity, though *C. elegans* will tolerate quite dry conditions.

Care Water regularly in summer, sparingly in winter. Provide good drainage; plants must never be allowed to become sodden or be left standing in water. Mist occasionally and sponge leaves with plain water from time to time. Give liquid feeds once a month during the growing season.

Potting on When the root ball is pushing its way out of the pot – usually every two or three years – repot using a peat-based compost, and make sure the soil is well firmed around the root ball.

Propagation From seed in spring, at a temperature of 24-27°C (75-80°F).

Problems Brown tips on the leaves may be caused by inadequate watering, or by insufficient moisture in the air. Plants grown in hot dry conditions need occasional misting. Brown spots on the leaves may be the result either of overwatering, or of watering with hard tap water. Brown leaves and rotting at the base is caused by waterlogging or poor drainage. Red spider mite and mealy bug are possible sources of trouble.

See also *Palms*, page 23-24.

CHLOROPHYTUM COMOSUM 'VARIEGATUM'

CHAMAEDOREA ELEGANS

CHLOROPHYTUM COMOSUM 'VARIEGATUM'
(Syn. C. CAPENSE, C. ELATUM)

South Africa
Spider plant
1m (3ft) or more

This well-known and easily grown plant is best suited to a hanging basket or pedestal, where the green and cream striped, grass-like leaves can arch in graceful profusion over the sides. Mature plants produce tiny white flowers and plantlets on long hanging stems. 'Variegatum' is the variety always sold.

Conditions Adaptable to a wide range of conditions, although it does best in a well lit position out of direct sun, which will fade the leaves. It needs moderate temperatures, not less than 7°C (45°F) in winter. Give plants some humidity, and mist regularly if the atmosphere is hot and dry.

Care Water liberally during spring and summer, and keep the compost barely moist in winter. Give weekly liquid feeds during the growing season.

Potting on Repot annually in spring; use a peat-based compost or John Innes No. 2

Propagation By division when repotting, or by pegging down plantlets into the soil and severing the runners once the roots are established. Put two or three plantlets in the same pot for a quick bushy display.

Problems Shrivelling and yellowing of leaves is usually caused by underwatering. Browning at the tips of the leaves may be the result of underfeeding or dry air, or be an indication that the plant needs repotting. Limp, pallid leaves may be due to overheating: keep plants away from direct sources of heat.

CHRYSANTHEMUM

CHRYSANTHEMUM

China and Japan
22·5-30cm (9-12in)

For growing as a houseplant the familiar garden perennial is usually 'dwarfed' by chemical treatment and artificially induced to flower out of season. It is best regarded as a temporary houseplant and discarded after flowering.

Conditions Position in good light to encourage the buds to open, but out of very strong sunlight. A cool temperature between 10 and 16°C (50-60°F) will keep the plants in flower longer.

Care during flowering Water thoroughly and water often – the compost should be constantly moist. The higher the temperature, the more water the plant will need.

Care after flowering Pot-grown chrysanthemums can be planted out in the garden after flowering where, if they survive at all, they will revert to their natural tall-growing habit.

Propagation It is possible to strike cuttings from plants after flowering, but only the professional will be able to provide the plant with the conditions required to induce flowering out of the normal season.

Problems Wilting and leaf fall indicate underwatering. The flowering period may be shortened if temperatures are too high, when the process of buds opening and flowering will be accelerated. If buds do not open this may be because a plant has not been 'brought on' enough in artificial conditions, so that buds are still green. Make sure buds are showing colour when buying plants.

CISSUS ANTARCTICA

Australia
Kangaroo vine
To 2·4m (8ft)

A rampant natural climber, kangaroo vine is related to the Virginia creeper (parthenocissus). The shiny green leaves are oval with serrated edges, and plants cling to their support by means of tendrils.

Conditions Grow in a position of indirect light or semi-shade. Year-round temperatures of 13-16°C (55-60°) are best, with a minimum of 10°C (50°F) and some additional humidity in the air in winter. Once established, plants should be kept in the same position, as they dislike change. Give support if growing as a climber.

Care From spring to autumn water thoroughly, allowing almost to dry out between waterings. Water very sparingly in winter. Mist the foliage regularly, especially in warm conditions, and give occasional liquid feeds during the growing season.

Pruning To obtain a shorter, bushier plant, pinch out leading shoots every now and then. Plants can be trimmed right back in spring if they have become too large for their position.

Potting on Repot annually in spring, in a loam-based compost (John Innes No. 2). Place a layer of broken crocks in the bottom of the pot to ensure good drainage. Plants kept down to a 15cm (6in) pot will seldom exceed 2m (6ft) in height.

Propagation By layering, or from stem cuttings of side shoots in spring.

Problems Brown patches on the leaves may be the result of exposure to sun. Shrivelled, yellowing and falling leaves indicate overwatering, and this may lead to rotting if not corrected. Brown dry foliage indicates lack of moisture in the air. Mildew on the leaves is a sign of waterlogging or inadequate drainage.

CISSUS ANTARCTICA

CLIVIA MINIATA

Natal
Kaffir lily
To 60cm (2ft)

Flowering bulbous plants for cool conditions, with showy, flame-coloured, trumpet-shaped flowers growing in umbels on stout stems throughout the spring and summer. The arching, strap-shaped leaves are a feature in themselves, and are more or less evergreen. As the plant matures the number of flowers increases annually, and red berries sometimes appear after the flowers. Clivias are undemanding and will withstand periods of neglect, provided they are not subjected to high temperatures.

Conditions During the summer keep pots in a position of light shade, such as an east-facing windowsill. Give the plants cool to average temperatures while they are flower-ing in summer. Rest them in an unheated room in winter at temperatures no higher than 10°C (50°F). Plants can be brought into flower earlier by increasing temperatures in January or February. Do not move plants once they are in bud or flower, and give them plenty of space, preferably away from other plants.

Care Water moderately in summer, allowing the compost to dry out slightly between waterings. Water very sparingly in winter – enough to prevent the compost from drying out completely. Give a liquid feed as the new leaves appear in summer, and sponge leaves occasionally.

Potting on Repot only when plants are literally growing out of their containers. Clivias flower best when pot-bound, and they resent root disturbance. Repotting may be necessary every two years for young plants, every four to five years for mature plants that have reached 25cm (10in) pots.

Propagation By division in spring; again the operation is best delayed until plants are in 25cm (10in) pots to sustain good flowering displays. The roots are easily damaged, and care must be taken when separating them; older plants, especially, will have developed thickly knotted root systems. Wash the old soil away before teasing them gently apart.

Problems Generally trouble-free.

See also the section on *Bulbs*, page 25-27.

CLIVIA MINIATA

CODIAEUM VARIEGATUM PICTUM

Malaysia
Joseph's coat
To 60cm (2ft)

A striking exotic foliage plant which comes in a wide variety of colours, ranging from pale yellows and greens to volcanic oranges and dark red-blacks. The leaf shape may be oval, lobed, narrow, straight or twisted. Other varieties include *C. reidii*, *C.* 'Mrs Iceton' and *C.* 'Golden Ring'.

Conditions This plant depends upon certain constant conditions for survival. These are full light with some sun, but protection from scorching sun which can damage the leaves; a constant warm temperature with a minimum of 16°C (60°F) in winter; protection from draughts and fluctuations of temperature; and finally a high degree of humidity. Keep the surrounding air moist by standing the plant in a shallow tray of damp gravel.

Care Water regularly and thoroughly during the growing season, using tepid water, and never allow the compost to dry out; mist daily. Water sparingly in winter. Give weekly liquid feeds during the growing season and sponge leaves with water to keep dust-free.

Potting on Repot when necessary, normally annually, in March; use a loam-based compost (John Innes No. 2).

Propagation From stem cuttings between March and June. Constant warm humid conditions are essential; a propagator gives most reliable results.

Problems Any problems that arise are likely to be due to unsuitable or inconstant conditions. Brown tips or edges on leaves indicate that the temperature is too low, or the atmosphere or compost is too dry. Fading leaf colour may be due to lack of light. Poor care and condition makes the plant susceptible to attack by red spider mite and scale insect.

CODIAEUM VARIEGATUM PICTUM

COFFEA ARABICA

COFFEA ARABICA

**Ethiopia
Coffee plant
To 1·2m (4ft)**

An attractive, bush-like foliage plant, with dark green, shiny, wavy-edged leaves. In its natural environment the coffee plant produces fragrant white flowers which open for only a brief period – less than 36 hours – and are followed by clusters of berries consisting of a fleshy outer cover that contains two seeds, each flattened on one side. Unfortunately, when grown as a houseplant it produces neither flowers nor seeds, but is well worth growing for its foliage.

Conditions Grow in a lightly shaded position away from direct summer sun, but allow more light in winter. Give a moderate temperature, minimum 10°C (50°F) in winter. The coffee plant will grow more vigorously in humid conditions, so either plunge the pot in damp peat or place on moistened pebbles.

Care Keep the compost moist at all times, and water more freely during the summer. Always use soft tepid water, or rainwater in hard water areas. Occasional spraying of leaves in summer will keep them shiny and improve general humidity. Pinch out the growing tips regularly to encourage bushy growth.

Potting on Repot when roots fill the pot – probably every two years. Use John Innes No. 2 potting compost with added peat, or a soil-less compost.

Propagation Grow coffee plants from seed in spring, or from cuttings of side shoots in late summer. Unroasted coffee beans will germinate if placed in moist peat and given a warm position – ideally in a propagator; beans that have been roasted stand no chance of germinating.

Problems Generally trouble-free if kept humid and away from draughts.

COLEUS BLUMEI

COLEUS BLUMEI

**Java
Flame nettle
To 45cm (1½ft)**

Bushy plants in a number of varieties, with colourful nettle-like leaves in variously patterned shades of green, yellow, bronze, purple and red. Unless the plant is a particularly fine healthy specimen, or can be kept in greenhouse conditions, Coleus is best treated as an annual and discarded in September, or kept over winter for cuttings the following spring. The flowers are best pinched out before they form to keep the plant in good shape.

Conditions Grow in a bright position with shading from midday sun to maintain good leaf colour. Give average temperatures with a minimum of 10°C (50°F) in winter, and some humidity.

Care Keep the compost moist during the growing season and mist occasionally; use rainwater whenever possible. If a plant is being kept over winter then reduce watering and keep on the dry side. Give weekly liquid feeds from June to September.

Pruning/trimming Pinch out the growing tips regularly to encourage bushiness. If the plant is being kept for a second season, prune back in February to about one-third its original size.

Potting on To bring coleus on to a good size during its brief lifespan in ordinary house conditions, pot on over the summer to a maximum pot size of 18cm (7in). Use John Innes No. 3 potting compost.

Propagation Grow from seed in January, or take stem cuttings in spring from particularly successful plants of the previous season. The latter is the only method guaranteed to produce plants to type. Maintain temperatures of 16-18°C (60-65°F).

Problems Usually the result of incorrect treatment. Leaf fall indicates a position in poor light. Straggly growth may also be due to poor light, or it may occur as a consequence of failure to pinch out the growing tips.

CORDYLINE TERMINALIS 'FIREBRAND'

CORDYLINE TERMINALIS 'FIREBRAND'

New Zealand
75cm (2½ft)

This plant is often confused with dracaena, to which it is very similar, and it is sometimes sold as *D. terminalis*. The long, glossy, spear-shaped leaves are mid-green flushed red or purple. The leaves grow upwards from a central point on the stem; the base of the stem may become more exposed as the plant matures and lower leaves are shed. *C.* 'Rededge' is smaller and more difficult.

Conditions Demands consistent conditions: a lightly shaded position out of contact with direct sun, but enough light to keep the leaves in good colour; a warm temperature of about 18°C (65°F) and not less than 13°C (55°F) in winter; and high humidity – pots should be kept plunged in containers filled with moist peat.

Care Water regularly, using rainwater or soft tepid water; keep the compost moist at all times, but avoid waterlogging. Reduce watering in winter, when overwatering can kill. Give a liquid feed every ten days during the growing season.

Potting on Pot on as necessary, using a peat-based soil-less compost.

Propagation In spring take 7·5cm (3in) stem cuttings from old leggy plants. Insert the section in a proprietary potting compost so that it is just covered. Keep at a temperature of 18-21°C (67-70°F), or use a heated propagator. When growth begins to sprout, pot on.

Problems Brown tips may be caused by inadequate humidity in the surrounding air, by dry compost or exposure to draughts. Curling of leaves occurs when temperatures are too low. Yellowing and falling of leaves is a natural part of the process of ageing – the plant will become increasingly leggy, and may eventually reach a point where it is best used for cuttings.

CRASSULA ARBORESCENS

South Africa
Jade plant
To 1m (3ft)

This branching succulent, which is related to the stonecrops and houseleeks, is like a miniature tree, with a smooth stem and fleshy grey-green leaves edged with red. Flowers are white, turning to red as they mature, and are borne in terminal clusters. *C. arborescens* needs warmth and regular exposure to sun in order to flower, and rarely does so in northern climates. However, it is an attractive plant, well worth growing for its delightful shape.

Conditions Grow on a sunny windowsill or similar bright position. It needs to be kept warm in summer and cooler in winter, minimum 7°C (45°F). Give ventilation in summer and stand outside when conditions are sufficiently hot and sunny.

Care Water regularly and thoroughly during the spring and summer, but avoid overwatering; allow the compost to dry out in between waterings. Keep on the dry side in winter, particularly when conditions are cool: the leaves will have stored a good deal

CRASSULA ARBORESCENS

of the previous summer's moisture and will be in little danger of suffering from dehydration. Give very weak liquid feeds of a high-potassium fertilizer once a fortnight during spring and summer.

Potting on Repot in April every second year, into the next pot size. Use a compost with good drainage, such as John Innes No. 2 with added coarse sand or grit. Shallow pots are best.

Propagation From leaf cuttings taken in spring and summer. Pull a leaf from the stem and allow it to dry out for a day before inserting it into the growing compost, or laying it flat on the surface, where it will root and eventually form new leaves around the base. Remove and pot up when well established. New plants can also be grown from 5-7·5cm (2-3in) stem cuttings taken in spring and summer, or from complete stems rooted in a sandy compost.

Problems Rotting at the base together with wilting of the plant top is probably due to overwatering or to poor drainage. Brown shrivelled patches on leaves indicate inadequate watering. White woolly patches on the leaves are caused by mealy bug.

See also *Cacti and Succulents*, page 21-22.

CTENANTHE OPPENHEIMIANA 'TRICOLOR'

Brazil
Never never plant
To 30cm (1ft)

Ctenanthes are very decorative foliage and specimen plants, closely related to the marantas and calatheas, though generally more difficult to care for in ordinary home conditions where humidity is lacking. *C. o.* 'Tricolor' has narrow pointed leaves, banded dark and light green, with cream splashes and maroon undersides. *C. lubbersiana* has dark green and yellow variegated leaves and is slightly easier, though less readily available.

Conditions The plants need a position in shade; the edges of the leaves will roll up in bright sunlight. A constant summer temperature of 21-24°C (70-75°F) is ideal, and not less than 18°C (65°F) in winter. A consistent high level of humidity is essential, and plant pots should be kept plunged in containers of moist peat. Bottle gardens provide the ideally balanced conditions.

Care Keep the compost constantly moist, using tepid soft water, and mist frequently. Give a weak liquid feed once a week from June to September.

Potting on Every two years in spring, in a peat-based potting compost.

Propagation By division when repotting. Keep new plants covered with polythene in a warm place until they are established.

Problems Curled or discoloured leaves are probably a result of overexposure to light. Brown dry leaf tips, leaf fall and poor growth can all be attributed to lack of humidity, which may also give rise to red spider mite. Dry yellowing leaves and leaf fall are due to inadequate watering, while limp and rotting stems are caused by overwatering in winter.

CTENANTHE OPPENHEIMIANA 'TRICOLOR'

CYCLAMEN PERSICUM

CYCLAMEN PERSICUM

Mediterranean regions
45cm (1½ft)

An autumn and winter-flowering tuberous pot plant, with green heart-shaped leaves, marbled silver. The flowers are white, pink or mauve, and are carried high above the plant on graceful fleshy stalks. Choose a plant with plenty of buds showing colour, and a few open flowers.

Conditions Grow in a well-lit position, with shade from excessive sun and out of draughts. Give a constant, moderately cool temperature, between 10 and 16°C (50-60°F). Some ventilation and moisture in the air will keep the plant healthy and in flower for the longest time. In centrally-heated and warm rooms, stand pots on damp gravel or in a container of moist peat.

Care during flowering Keep the compost moist, but do not overwater or allow the plant to stand directly in water. Either water from the top and around the edges rather than into the centre of the plant, or use the immersion method (see page 116). Drain thoroughly before replacing on the saucer. Mist leaves regularly, but keep the flowers dry. Give weekly feeds until the plant is in full flower. Twist off dead flowers and any yellowed leaves from the base of the plant, leaving no bits of stalk.

Care after flowering After flowering water moderately until the leaves turn yellow, and reduce watering as they die back. Place the pot on its side in a cool, dark, frost-free spot; water occasionally until the new shoots begin to appear in June or July, and pot on.

Potting on Move into the next pot size: pot-bound conditions encourage flowering. Use a loam-based compost and bury the corm to half its depth. Keep in a shaded spot. Gradually increase watering, and give a weak liquid feed every two or three weeks. As the buds appear, from about September on, move to a lighter spot.

Propagation From seed, sown in January or February to flower the following winter.

Problems Overwatering or waterlogging can cause rotting or collapse. Lime-yellow foliage and a short flowering period indicate either conditions that are too hot and dry, or incorrect watering. Curled or stunted leaves may be due to cyclamen mite. Grey mould on leaves and crown indicates botrytis disease: remove dead leaves and flowers immediately.

CYPERUS ALTERNIFOLIUS

Africa
Umbrella plant
75cm (2½ft) or more

These plants have tall green stems, and bear umbrella-like grassy bracts and greeny-yellow flowers. They are water plants, and require a degree of moisture that would be fatal to most other houseplants.

Conditions Provide a bright position away from direct sun. Will tolerate a temperature range between 10 and 20°C (50-68°F), and grows happily in unheated rooms. Roots and compost need to be kept continually wet or standing in shallow water.

Care Stand the plant in a bowl of water which is always kept topped up; mist leaves frequently. Feed once a week throughout the year. Cut out yellowing stems to encourage new growth.

Potting on Repot annually in a loam-based compost (John Innes No. 2).

Propagation By division when repotting, or by detaching a flower head with young shoot on a short piece of stem, and inserting the shoot into wet soil. Alternatively, bend the whole stem over and insert the shoot into soil; separate from the parent when established.

Problems Brown tips are most likely to be caused by insufficient water or dry air, or to indicate that the plant needs repotting.

CYPERUS ALTERNIFOLIUS

CYRTOMIUM FALCATUM

Provide moderate to warm temperatures in summer, cooler in winter, with a minimum of 7°C (45°F). Mist the leaves regularly. Cyrtomiums are hardy in sheltered areas and can be planted out of doors, but keep indoor specimens away from sources of direct heat, including sun, and for best results keep the atmosphere humid.

Care Water freely in spring and summer, sparingly in autumn and winter, and give monthly liquid feeds during the growing season.

Potting on Repot every second or third year in spring, using an ordinary potting compost with added leaf mould.

Propagation By division of the crown in March or April.

Problems Generally trouble-free, provided the leaves are not exposed to direct sun and the plant is not overwatered during the winter months.

See also *Ferns*, Page 13-14.

CYRTOMIUM FALCATUM
(Syn. POLYSTICHUM FALCATUM)

South-east Asia
Holly fern
30-60cm (1-2ft)

A handsome fern with long, glossy, dark green fronds composed of pointed leaflets arranged in pairs. *C. f.* 'Rochfordianum' is smaller than the type, growing to about 30cm (1ft), and has larger leaflets with wavy, holly-like margins. It is a very amenable houseplant, tolerating dryer conditions than most ferns.

Conditions Grow in a shaded position and allow some ventilation during the summer.

DAVALLIA CANARIENSIS

**Spain, North Africa, Canary Islands
Hare's foot fern
30-45cm (1-1½ft)**

The furry rhizomes of this delicate fern grow around the edge of the pot on the soil surface and hang down over the edge, looking like animals' paws. Davallias are seen at their best when grown in a hanging basket, where their attractive, deeply cut fronds can arch over the sides. Among the ferns, *D. canariensis* is one of the more tolerant of dry house conditions.

Conditions Grow in good indirect light, on a north- or east-facing windowsill. Temperatures should be average to warm, with a winter minimum of 7°C (45°F). Although davallias are tolerant houseplants, it is best to maintain a humid atmosphere by misting around the plant when conditions are hot and dry.

Care Water to keep compost moist in summer, less frequently in cooler winter conditions. Keep well drained. Give a fortnightly liquid feed during the growing season, and remove any dead or damaged fronds as soon as they appear.

Potting on Repot in spring when roots fill the pot, using equal quantities of John Innes No. 2 potting compost and peat, or equal parts moss peat, peat-based compost and sharp sand. Leave the rhizomes exposed.

Propagation The surface-rooting rhizomes may be pinned down to the compost. Pot on when the roots are established, using the usual compost.

Problems Generally due to incorrect treatment. Yellowing fronds with brown tips, and fronds dying back are caused by high temperatures and dry air. Limp, wilting, yellowing fronds indicate overwatering; plants must never be allowed to become waterlogged.

See also *Ferns*, page 13-14.

DAVALLIA CANARIENSIS

DIEFFENBACHIA PICTA 'EXOTICA'

**South America
Dumb cane
To 1m (3ft)**

An attractive foliage plant that needs some care if it is to be seen at its best. Large oval leaves grow upwards from fleshy stems to a length of 30cm (1ft), and are dark green splashed with cream. The sap of the plant is poisonous.

Conditions Grow in a semi-shaded position away from draughts in summer; allow more light in winter. Give constant warmth with a winter minimum temperature of 16°C (60°F), and a high level of humidity in the air. Keep pots in containers of moist peat.

Care Water regularly and well in summer, but allow the compost to dry out slightly on the surface so as to avoid waterlogging around the stem, as this may cause rotting.

Keep surrounding peat continually moist. Decrease watering in winter. Mist leaves regularly, and feed once a fortnight during the growing season.

Potting on Repot annually in spring, using a rich potting compost (John Innes No. 3).

Propagation In spring, cut the topmost growing shoot of the plant with a 7·5cm (3in) section of stem attached, and insert this in the growing compost. When the growing tip has been removed, small shoots will develop at the base of the plant, and these can also be detached and potted up. Warm moist conditions are essential. After handling cuttings take care to wash off all traces of the sap, and in any case do not bring this into contact with the mouth.

Problems Usually due to incorrect treatment. Limp stems and discoloured foliage are probably due to overwatering and/or low temperatures. Wilting, yellowing and falling leaves are likely to be the result of insufficient warmth and humidity.

DIZYGOTHECA ELEGANTISSIMA

Australasia
False aralia
To 1·2m (4ft)

A fine and graceful specimen plant with delicate, deeply serrated leaflets arranged in finger-like groups and rising from an upright central stem. The leaves emerge coppery-red and turn dark green as they mature. It is not a particularly easy plant to grow.

Conditions Grow in a lightly shaded position and out of draughts. It needs constant warmth and humidity, with a minimum winter temperature of 15°C (59°F). Avoid fluctuations of temperature as far as possible, and, for additional humidity, group together with other plants needing similar conditions.

Care Water moderately in spring and summer and sparingly in winter, but never allow

DIEFFENBACHIA PICTA 'EXOTICA'

the root ball to dry out. Mist the plant and the surrounding air frequently. Give fortnightly liquid feeds from spring to late summer.

Pruning As plants mature they lose their delicate form. Pinch out growing tips during winter dormancy to encourage juvenile growth.

Potting on Repot every two years in the spring, using a rich loam-based compost (John Innes No. 3).

Propagation From seed or stem cuttings in spring, but not easy.

Problems Most likely to arise from incorrect treatment. Falling lower leaves are probably due to insufficient light and/or dry air. Ungainly growth can be improved by cutting back the stem in early spring to encourage new growth.

DIZYGOTHECA ELEGANTISSIMA

Dracaena

The dracaenas are ornamental foliage plants, mainly tall-growing with long narrow leaves rising directly from a central stem. Many forms have a natural tendency to shed their lower leaves as the plant grows to maturity, leaving a tuft of leaves on the upper stem which gives a palm-like appearance. They are best 'stopped' at between 90 and 120cm (3-4ft) before they become too ungainly. *D. godseffiana* is exceptional in having a low-growing, branched and bushy habit. All prefer average to warm conditions with some surrounding humidity, but react badly to waterlogging and direct contact with wet soil.

Dracaena deremensis

**Tropical Africa
Striped dracaena
To 1·2m (4ft)**

Dracaena deremensis

The upright, arching leaves are sword-shaped, green and white striped, and grow to a length of 45cm (1½ft). There are many varieties, some with alternate green and white or silver stripes, others with a central band of white and green leaf margins.

Conditions Grow in a position of light shade. Temperatures should be warm, not less than 18°C (65°F) in spring and summer, 13°C (55°F) in winter. A high degree of humidity is needed; pots should be kept plunged in containers of moist peat, and the leaves misted regularly.

Care Water the compost thoroughly but carefully in summer, more sparingly in winter, and keep peat containers continually moist. These plants do best in conditions of surrounding moisture, since direct contact with wet or waterlogged soil tends to bring about premature leaf fall. Give a liquid feed every two weeks from June to September.

Potting on Repot every other year in April, using a rich loam compost with added peat, or John Innes No. 3. Keep the pot size down to 15-17·5cm (6-7in) for as long as possible.

Propagation From basal shoots, or from the growing tip, taken with 7·5cm (3in) of stem and rooted in a mixture of peat and sand at a temperature of 21°C (70°F).

Problems Usually due to lack of humidity. Loss of lower leaves occurs naturally with age, but may be hastened by overwatering.

Dracaena godseffiana 'Florida Beauty'

**Central Africa
Gold dust dracaena
60cm (2ft)**

A shrubby, branching plant with dark green, laurel-like leaves heavily flecked with yellow. As a small plant it can be grown in a bottle garden, though it is not intolerant of drier home conditions.

Conditions Give a position in good light to keep strong leaf variegation. Temperatures should be moderate in summer, with a minimum of 10°C (50°F) in winter. Give some humidity by misting occasionally, but avoid overwetting the leaves.

Care Water moderately to keep compost moist, but never sodden, between May and September. During the rest of the year water only enough to prevent the compost from drying out. Give a liquid feed once a fortnight during the summer.

Potting on Pot on in April every other year, using a rich, well-drained, loam-based compost (John Innes No. 3).

Propagation From tip cuttings taken with three or four leaves attached. Insert in equal parts peat and sand in a temperature of 21-24°C (70-75°F). A heated propagator will give best results.

Problems Stunted growth may be caused by root mealy bugs: check for evidence around the roots. Avoid overwatering.

DRACAENA GODSEFFIANA

DRACAENA MARGINATA

Tropical Africa
To 1·5m (5ft) or more

An elegant specimen plant with long, fine, red-margined leaves growing from a narrow central stem. *D. m.* 'Tricolor' has leaves attractively variegated with green, cream and pink, and is slightly more difficult to grow.

Conditions Grow in a position with sufficient light to maintain the leaf variegations, but with shading from direct sun. Provide warm to moderate temperatures, with a winter minimum of between 10 and 13°C (50-55°F). *D. marginata* is more tolerant of an ordinary home environment than most dracaenas, but avoid cold wet winter conditions.

Care From spring to autumn water to keep the compost moist but never waterlogged. Reduce watering in winter. Provide some humidity by misting the leaves regularly, and give occasional liquid feeds during the growing season.

Pruning Pinch out the growing tip at a height of about 60cm (2ft) to prevent the plant becoming too leggy.

Potting on Pot on every other year in a loamy compost, firming the soil around the root ball.

Propagation From young shoots which may be produced along the stem, or from the growing tip as for *D. deremensis*.

Problems Yellowing of leaves and premature leaf drop are most likely to be caused by cold damp conditions and waterlogging around the roots. Loss of leaf colour indicates insufficient light.

DRACAENA MARGINATA

DRACAENA SANDERIANA

but provide some humidity by misting around the plant. Keep away from windows on cold nights.

Care Water well between May and September, sparingly from September to early November and March to May, and keep almost dry in the winter. Give fortnightly liquid feeds from May to September.

Potting on Every other year in April until the plant has reached the height you want, using John Innes No. 3 potting compost. Thereafter keep to the same pot size, and top-dress every other year.

Propagation From tip cuttings of mature growths. Insert in equal quantities of peat and sand and place in a propagator at a temperature of 21-24°C (70-75°F). The first leaves will be true green; coloured leaves are produced within a few months. Place in 7·5cm (3in) pots of John Innes No. 1 potting compost once the roots are established.

Problems As for *D. marginata*.

EPIPHYLLUM × ACKERMANNII

Central and South America
Orchid cactus
60-90cm (2-3ft)

Epiphytic forest cacti with long, trailing, flattened stems that look like leaves. Large, bell-shaped, sometimes fragrant flowers in brilliant colours grow directly from the edge of the stem on the upper part of the plant, usually in late spring and early summer. The *ackermannii* hybrids in shades of red are the easiest to buy and flower. Named hybrids in other colours may have to be bought from specialist nurseries. Give the long stems some support.

Conditions Grow in a well-lit position, shaded from direct sun, such as a north or east-facing windowsill. Temperatures need to be warm in summer, cooler in winter, with a minimum of 13°C (55°F). Provide humidity by frequent misting in summer, and give good ventilation. Plants can be

DRACAENA SANDERIANA

Zaire
Ribbon plant
45cm (1½ft) or more

A compact form which bears foliage evenly and densely up a non-branching stem. The comparatively small ribbon-like, grey-green leaves have ivory-coloured, wavy edges. It will grow to a height of 2m (6ft) in a 25cm (10in) pot, but stays more compact if kept in a 12·5cm (5in) pot.

Conditions Grow in good light to encourage leaf variegation, but avoid direct sun. Give moderate temperatures, with a winter minimum of 10°C (50°F). *D. sanderiana* is generally more tolerant of dry centrally-heated conditions than other dracaenas;

kept outside in a shaded spot after flowering is over in midsummer, and brought back inside in September.

Care Water thoroughly and regularly when the plants are in flower and actively growing. Reduce watering in the autumn. In winter, until the buds form, keep plants on the dry side, but never allow them to dry out completely. Do not move the plants once the buds have formed. Give fortnightly liquid feeds with a high-potassium fertilizer from bud development until early autumn.

Potting on Repot annually after flowering in an ordinary potting compost with added leaf mould, and small quantites of bone meal as described in the section on *Cacti and succulents* (page 21). Alternatively use John Innes No. 2 potting compost.

Propagation From seed in April, at a temperature of 21°C (70°F), or from stem cuttings taken in late spring and early summer and allowed to dry out for several days before being potted into the plant's usual growing compost.

Problems Generally trouble-free, provided they are given sufficient water during the growing period and allowed to rest in cooler, dry conditions.

EPIPHYLLUM × ACKERMANNII

EUONYMUS JAPONICUS

EUONYMUS JAPONICUS

Europe
Spindle tree
To 2m (6ft)

A hardy garden plant which makes an attractive houseplant when grown in a cool, well-ventilated place. It has freely branching stems with narrow, oval, leathery leaves. *E. j.* 'Aurea' has glossy, golden-yellow leaves. There are several variegated forms. *E. j. microphyllus* has either green and yellow or green and white variegated leaves, less than 1cm (½in) in length, and is generally a more compact plant. *E. j. ovatus* 'Aurea' has dark green leaves with yellow margins.

Conditions Grow in a bright, well ventilated area, shaded from direct sunlight. Maintain a cool temperature with a winter minimum of 7°C (45°F). Place outside in the summer, or ventilate well.

Care Water freely during the growing season but sparingly in the winter. Sponge the leaves regularly and give monthly liquid feeds from spring to autumn. Remove the plain leaves on variegated forms to retain variegation.

Pruning Check growth by cutting well back in spring.

Potting on When necessary, repot in spring in John Innes No. 3 potting compost. Mature plants should be top-dressed annually. Oversized plants may be moved to a permanent position in the garden.

Problems Leaf drop in winter is the result of high temperatures. Red spider is sometimes a problem.

EUPHORBIA MILLII SPLENDENS

EUPHORBIA MILII SPLENDENS

Madagascar
Crown of thorns
30-60cm (1-2ft)

A flowering succulent from the same family as the poinsettia, but very different in appearance. Bright green, fleshy oval leaves are produced at the tips of thick branching stems which are covered with sharp thorns. Small scarlet flowers appear in the leaf axils, and may last for many months.

Conditions Grow in a bright sunny position with warm to moderate temperatures, not less than 13°C (55°F) in winter. Give good ventilation in summer or place outside.

Care Water moderately from spring until autumn, sparingly in winter. Allow the soil surface to dry out in between waterings. Like most succulents it stores water in the leaves and is tolerant of dry air.

Potting on Pot on every other year in summer, or when necessary, in a well-drained loam compost with plenty of sand or grit.

Propagation Use tip cuttings taken from old branches. It is a good idea to wear gloves to protect your hands from contact with the spines, since not only are they very sharp, but if broken away from the stem will exude a milky sap which is poisonous and causes severe skin irritation.

Problems Generally trouble-free.

See also *Cacti and Succulents*, pages 21-22.

EUPHORBIA PULCHERRIMA

Mexico
Poinsettia
30-45cm (1-1½ft)

This favourite winter-flowering pot plant has broad, bright green leaves and brightly coloured decorative bracts with tiny yellow-white flowers at the centre. The bracts are usually scarlet, but pale pink or white forms are also available. The sap from the plant is poisonous.

Conditions Give a draught-free position in full light, where the plant can receive any winter sun available. Daytime temperatures should be between 13 and 18°C (55-65°F), with a minimum at night of 10°C (50°F). Keep pots plunged in containers of moist peat, and do not expose to gas fumes.

Care during flowering Water carefully, allowing the soil almost to dry out between waterings. Use the leaves as an indicator and water well as soon as any sign of wilting is observed.

Care after flowering Plants are usually discarded after flowering, but it is possible

EUPHORBIA PULCHERRIMA

(though not particularly easy) to keep and bring them into flower again the following year. To be brought into bud, plants require alternating periods of darkness and light corresponding to the length of night and day in their native habitat. If plants are exposed to artificial light when daylight is over, the result will be leaf and stem growth at the expense of flower head development. When flowering is finished, cut the plant back to 10cm (4in) from the base and stop watering. Place in a shady spot, and water only to prevent from drying out completely. When new shoots appear, resume watering and either pot on or remove some of the old soil, returning the plant to the same pot with added loam-based compost (John Innes No. 2). Give fortnightly liquid feeds from now on until autumn when the new bracts appear.

From September until about the end of November, place the plants in a bright position where they will receive only natural daylight. Alternatively, cover them with a black plastic bag from early evening for about 14 hours. Once the new flowering bracts appear, treat as before.

Propagation By cuttings from the tips of new growth, taken in summer.

Problems Generally trouble-free if given enough light and not overwatered. Loss of flower heads and browning of the leaf edges indicate insufficient humidity: correct this by misting.

EXACUM AFFINE

**Island of Socotra
Persian violet
20-30cm (9-12in)**

A neat, bushy, free-flowering plant which has small shiny heart-shaped leaves and masses of tiny fragrant blue flowers with yellow stamens. These will cover the plant from about July to October. Exacum is a biennial which is best grown from seed each year and discarded after flowering.

Conditions Place in a bright position with shading from bright sunlight. Cool to moderate temperatures, between 13 and 16°C (55-60°F), will keep the plant in flower for the longest possible time.

Care Keep the compost moist at all times, and mist the leaves occasionally, particularly in warm temperatures. Give a weak liquid feed once a fortnight. Pinch out the growing tips from time to time.

Potting on Plants can sometimes be successfully overwintered. Pot on into a loam-based compost (John Innes No. 2) in spring.

Propagation From seed sown in March or August. Summer-sown seeds will produce sturdier plants, ready for flowering the following year, but the seedlings must be overwintered at a minimum temperature of 16°C (60°F) to survive.

Problems Generally trouble-free.

EXACUM AFFINE

× FATSHEDERA LIZEI

Garden hybrid
Ivy tree
To 1·8m (6ft) or more

A plant for either the garden or the house, the ivy tree is a hybrid of two separate genera, *Fatsia japonica* and *Hedera helix*. The majority of hybrids are raised from species within the same genus, but this attractive and hardy plant combines some of the best features of the castor oil plant *Fatsia* and that excellent outdoor standby, the ivy *Hedera*. This parentage is reflected in the position of the '×' at the beginning of the name. Shiny, lobed, deep green leaves grow out from stout, rather floppy stems. Pale green flowers sometimes appear in the autumn. The plant naturally forms a robust climber which will grow rapidly up a support such as a staircase, but can be kept as a tall bushy specimen by constant pinching out of the growing tips. The variegated form has cream marks on the leaf.

Conditions Grow in a light or partly shaded position, out of direct sunlight. Fatshedera prefers cool conditions and will grow quite happily in winter temperatures as low as 1·5°C (35°F), provided it is protected from draughts.

Care Water freely in spring and summer, sparingly in winter, but do not allow the roots to dry out. Mist and wipe the leaves occasionally with a damp sponge to keep free of dust.

Potting on Repot annually in spring, in a loam-based compost (John Innes No. 2) and pinch out the growing tips at the same time.

Propagation From stem cuttings taken from the top part of the plant in July or August, or from a single leaf with part of the stem attached.

Problems Browning of the leaf edges may occur due to overwatering. Loss of lower leaves indicates conditions which are too hot and dry.

× FATSHEDERA LIZEI

FATSIA JAPONICA
(Syn. ARALIA SIEBOLDII)

Japan
Castor oil plant
To 1m (3ft) or more

A handsome foliage plant for the house or garden, with large, lobed, glossy, mid-green leaves which stand well out from the strong central stem.

Conditions Grow in a light or semi-shaded position out of direct sun. Temperatures should be kept low, with a winter minimum of 7°C (45°F), and 10°C (50°F) for the variegated form. Fatsia will tolerate temperatures up to 21°C (70°F), but is happiest in cool, well-ventilated conditions.

Care Water well from spring to autumn, sparingly in winter. Mist leaves of plants growing in warm temperatures and give regular fortnightly feeds during the growing season. Sponge the leaves occasionally to keep them free of dust. The variegated form is less hardy.

Pruning Curious green flower heads appear on mature plants and, as they do not particularly improve the appearance of the plant, are best removed. Pinch out growing tips in spring to maintain vigorous growth and a full and bushy shape.

Potting on Pot on annually in spring using a loam-based compost (John Innes No. 2), until a 20cm (8in) pot is reached. Thereafter top-dress annually in spring.

Problems Shrivelled leaves are the result of hot dry air or direct sun. Yellowing and drooping of leaves is a result of overwatering. Pale spotted leaves with dry edges indicate underwatering; a large plant will need frequent watering in summer.

FICUS BENJAMINA

India
Weeping fig
90-180cm (3-6ft) or more

A graceful indoor tree with light green, slender-pointed leaves hanging from arching stems, and delicate, slightly pendulous side branches. As the plant matures the leaves turn a darker green and the pale grey trunk becomes silvery-grey. An excellent specimen plant.

Conditions Grow in a brightly lit position, away from direct sun and draughts. Provide moderate, even temperatures, with a minimum of 13°C (55°F), and keep from contact with radiators and other sources of direct heat. Maintain a humid atmosphere by plunging the pot in damp peat or setting on moist pebbles. Support may be needed as the plant matures.

Care Keep the soil evenly moist in summer, using tepid rainwater if possible in hard water areas, and allow the compost to dry out slightly in between waterings. Water sparingly in winter, while the plant is resting. In hot dry conditions mist the leaves frequently, and clean them regularly with damp cotton wool. Give a weak liquid feed every 10-14 days from May to September. Do not move the plant unless abso-

FICUS BENJAMINA

lutely necessary, as this invariably results in the loss of some leaves.

Potting on This should normally be every two years, in a peat-based compost with a little extra sand added, or John Innes No. 2. Tall specimens may become top-heavy, but the use of a clay rather than plastic pot will increase stability.

Propagation From 5-10cm (2-4in) cuttings of side shoots between April and June, rooted in a propagator; or by air layering from May to July.

Problems Some lower leaves will naturally be lost during the rest period, but others will also fall if there is a sudden change in temperature, or the plant is moved. Abundant leaf-loss may be due to inadequate light. Wilting is the result of underwatering. In dry conditions red spider mite or mealy bug may attack – mist the plant regularly and increase humidity.

FATSIA JAPONICA

FICUS ELASTICA 'ROBUSTA'

FICUS ELASTICA 'ROBUSTA'

Tropical Asia
Rubber plant
To 2·4m (8ft)

A handsome and popular plant, with large, leathery, shiny dark green leaves which are oval-shaped and grow from a single stem. The leaves first appear covered with a red sheath and this colouring is retained by the young leaves for a short period.

Conditions Grow in a well-lit position away from direct sun. Temperatures should be moderate, with a winter minimum of 13°C (55°F). Avoid lower or fluctuating temperatures, which will result in leaf drop and an unsightly length of bare stem at the base of the plant. Provide some humidity by misting the plant occasionally.

Care Water freely in summer with tepid water, but allow compost to become almost dry in between waterings. Water sparingly in winter. Wipe the leaves with a damp sponge regularly to avoid any build-up of dust, which will restrict the growth of the plant. Give fortnightly liquid feeds. When the plant has reached a height of 1·8m (6ft), side shoots may be encouraged by removal of the growing tip.

Potting on If necessary, pot on in May. Ficus are generally more vigorous in small pots.

Propagation By air layering; see page 126

Problems Red spider mite and mealy bug may attack the plant. Sudden loss of leaves is caused by overwatering, low temperatures or lack of light. Dry shrivelling leaves indicate underwatering, lack of humidity or exposure to direct sun.

FICUS LYRATA

West Africa
Fiddle leaf fig
To 1·2m (4ft)

The distinctively large, wavy-edged, violin-shaped leaves of this plant are a glossy mid-green and sometimes have golden-yellow markings. It is a sparsely branched plant, which is most effective when growing in a group with smaller-leaved specimens.

Conditions Needs a shady spot away from direct sun, and constant warmth – not less than 16°C (60°F) in winter. It prefers a humid atmosphere, which will be partially provided by other plants if it is growing in a group, but sinking the pot in damp peat will also be of benefit to the plant.

Care Water freely during the summer, but to avoid waterlogging, allow the compost to dry out slightly in between waterings. Water sparingly in winter, and always use tepid soft water. Mist frequently to increase humidity, and sponge the leaves occasionally with a damp sponge. Feed with a liquid solution of fertilizer every 10-14 days from May to September. In warm weather provide plenty of ventilation.

Potting on Only when absolutely necessary, pot on into the next pot size. It is important to restrict root growth, since the plant has a tendency to become leggy.

Propagation By air layering; see page 126.

Problems Red spider mite and mealy bug may attack. Sudden leaf loss may be the result of an atmosphere which is too dry, underwatering or exposure to direct sun.

FICUS PUMILA

China
Creeping fig
Spread to 60cm (2ft)

The creeping or trailing fig is a delicate little creeper which grows well in a hanging basket or as ground cover under larger plants, although it is not very adaptable and, if used in mixed groups with other houseplants, will impose its particular requirements on the rest. It has papery-thin, heart-shaped leaves that do not retain moisture in the way that fleshier leaves can, and which will therefore tolerate neither sunshine nor general neglect. It has thin, wiry stems, and these develop aerial hairs which will cling to any rough surface. It is a good plant for a bottle garden.

Conditions Grows best in a shady position with moderate temperatures, and a minimum of 7°C (45°F) in winter. At its best when rambling over a moist pebble bed, *F. pumila* must have a humid atmosphere and should be misted regularly. Keep pots standing on shallow trays of gravel, and do not let these dry out.

Care Provide compost that is evenly moist throughout the year, otherwise the leaves will shrivel and die. Give a liquid feed every two weeks in the growing season. Growing tips should be regularly pinched out in the early stages of growth to encourage branching side shoots.

Potting on When the roots fill the pot – normally every two years – pot on in spring. Use a peat-based potting compost.

Propagation Take cuttings from side shoots between April and June, and root these in a heated propagator.

Problems Red spider mite and mealy bug are often a problem. Poor overall health is usually a consequence of failure to meet this fussy plant's requirements. Dry shrivelled leaves are caused by underwatering, insufficient humidity or exposure to sun.

FICUS LYRATA

FICUS PUMILA

FITTONIA ARGYRONEURA 'NANA'

FITTONIA ARGYRONEURA 'NANA'

Peru
Snakeskin plant
Spread 15cm (6in) or more

A low-growing plant which forms an intricate network of leaves over the entire surface of its pot. The tiny, paper-thin, oval leaves have white 'fish-bone' vein markings. Easier than *F. argyroneura* and *F. verschaffeltii*, which are only suitable for the bottle garden or terrarium, *F. a.* 'Nana' is more tolerant of slightly drier air and will provide colourful ground cover for group arrangements, as well as in a bottle garden.

Conditions Grow well away from direct sun. Give constant warmth all year round, with a minimum temperature of 16°C (60°F), and provide humidity by setting pot-grown plants in moist peat. Avoid exposure to draughts.

Care Water regularly throughout the growing season using tepid water, and aim to keep the compost evenly moist, never waterlogged. Water cautiously in winter, when overwatering can cause stem rot. Mist frequently, and give monthly feeds of liquid fertilizer.

Potting on Normally annually in spring when the roots fill the pot. Use a peat-based soil-less compost and a shallow pot.

Propagation Stems will grow naturally over the side of the pot and root themselves in the surrounding peat. Separate rooted stems from the parent plant, and pot up.

Problems Yellowing and wilting leaves are the result of overwatering – remove the root ball from the pot and examine the roots: root surgery will be possible if they are still white, but first leave the plant out of its pot for two days to allow the compost to dry slightly. Cold wet conditions will result in plant collapse during winter. Shrivelling leaves are caused by either lack of humidity or too much light.

GARDENIA JASMINOIDES 'FLORIDA'

China
To 1m (3ft)

A shapely shrub with glossy, dark green leaves growing in whorls of three around long stems. Exquisitely fragrant, waxy-white, double blooms are formed singly from the leaf axils at the tips of the shoots. 'Fortuniana' is another outstanding form with solitary, white, heavily scented flowers, 7·5cm (3in) across. The main flowering period is from June to August, but 'Veitchiana' flowers in winter. The plants are lime-hating and need acid soil.

Conditions Grow in bright light away from direct sun. To grow gardenias successfully,

GARDENIA JASMINOIDES

two levels of temperature are necessary. During active growth daytime temperatures of 21-27°C (70-80°F) and night-time temperatures of 16-18°C (60-65°F) will encourage flower formation. Keep between 10 and 16°C (50-60°F) during the dormant period. Established plants may be plunged in peat out of doors from late June to mid-September. Ventilate well when the temperature exceeds 18°C (65°F) if the plant remains indoors. In winter keep away from radiators, and avoid draughts.

Care Keep summer-flowering plants just moist in winter, but water winter-flowering varieties freely. Summer-flowering forms should be watered freely while in active growth, and the surrounding air misted with tepid water, but avoid spraying blooms directly. The lime content in hard tap water will turn leaves yellow: use rainwater whenever possible, or give occasional watering with sequestrene. Give a liquid feed every four weeks during the growing season but more frequently when buds appear, to encourage flowering. Pinch out growing tips regularly to encourage the plant to form a good shape and vigorous growth. Nipping out of early buds will help to induce later flowering.

Care after flowering Cut back all shoots by one-half to two-thirds.

Repotting Pot on in spring when the pot is full of roots; use a peat-based compost with a little crushed charcoal, and repot at the same level as before.

Propagation Take stem cuttings of non-flowering shoots with a heel in early summer, and root in equal quantities of sand and peat. Place in a propagator at a temperature of 18-21°C (65-70°F).

Problems Generally the result of incorrect treatment. Yellowing leaves are the result of careless watering and too little iron. Bud drop may be caused by sudden changes in temperature or by incorrect watering. Red spider mite may be a problem where humidity is low.

GREVILLEA ROBUSTA

GREVILLEA ROBUSTA

New South Wales
Silk oak
To 1m (3ft) or more

An elegant small tree with delicate feathery foliage. It will grow to 2m (6ft) or more, but as the plant matures the mid-green leaves become a rather dull dark green, and once the plant has reached 1m (3ft) it is better discarded.

Conditions Grow in a bright and well-ventilated position out of direct sun in the summer; in winter give maximum light. Temperatures should be cool, with a winter minimum of 7°C (45°F). If possible place outside during the summer.

Care Water freely during the summer, never allowing the root ball to dry out, and sparingly in the winter. Always use rainwater in hard water areas; grevilleas are lime-haters and must have an acid environment. Give a fortnightly liquid feed between May and September. Occasional watering with sequestrene may also be necessary, particularly in hard water areas. Remove older leaves as they turn brown.

Potting on Repot annually in spring, using a peat-based compost.

Propagation Easily grown from seed sown in spring.

Problems Plant collapse is normally caused by overwatering or by high temperatures.

GUZMANIA LINGULATA

GUZMANIA LINGULATA

South America
To 45cm (1½ft)

A group of mainly epiphytic bromeliads with brilliantly coloured flowering bracts and glossy leaves which form a water retaining vase. *G. lingulata* has green, sword-shaped leaves arranged in a wide-based rosette, and a flowering spike composed of crimson bracts which rises to a height of 30cm (1ft) from the centre of the plant, and is surmounted by a cluster of small yellow flowers. These plants need warmth and a high degree of humidity.

Conditions Grow in a permanent position of light shade. It needs warm temperatures all year round, minimum 18°C (65°F), and constant high humidity. Mist frequently with tepid softened water, and keep pots plunged in containers of moist peat.

Care Keep the central vase topped up with water, ideally rainwater; empty and refill it every three to four months. Keep the compost moist in summer, and on the dry side in winter. The plants can be given occasional feeds in the spring and summer, either in the form of a foliar spray, or as a weak liquid solution added to the water in the vase, but not when the plant is in flower.

Potting on Repot into the next pot size every two or three years, or when the roots have filled the pot. Use a mixture of equal parts peat, sphagnum moss and sand.

Propagation From offsets produced at the base of the plant and detached, with some roots, when they are one-third to half the size of the parent plant. Allow them to dry for a few days before potting them up individually in the growing compost.

Problems Brown patches on the leaves may be caused by direct exposure to sun. Brown tips on the leaves usually indicate insufficient humidity in the air.

GYNURA SARMENTOSA

India
Velvet plant
60cm (2ft)

A vigorous trailing plant which is at its best in a hanging container. The dark green, roughly triangular leaves may be shallowly lobed. The stems and leaves are covered with the velvet-like, dark red-purplish hairs which give the plant its popular name. Dandelion-like flowers appear in spring, and should be instantly removed, as they have an extremely unpleasant smell. The plant will tend to become uncontrollably straggly after two to three years, and is better discarded and new plants grown on from easily propagated cuttings.

Conditions In summer grow in a light place away from direct sun, but give maximum light in winter to encourage good leaf colour. Give moderate temperatures, minimum 13°C (55°F) in winter, though higher temperatures will be tolerated. Gynura can also be grown as a climber.

Care Water liberally in summer and keep the compost barely moist in winter. Mist leaves occasionally, but avoid getting them too wet as they are easily damaged. Give fortnightly liquid feeds from May to September. Encourage side shoots by regularly pinching out the growing tips, and remove any straggly stems in spring.

Potting on In April or May if the plant is pot-bound. Use John Innes No. 2 or a soil-less compost.

Propagation From cuttings of firm shoots taken in March or April. Pot up three plants to a 25cm (10in) basket.

Problems Pests and diseases are rare.

HAWORTHIA MARGARITIFERA

South Africa
To 15cm (6in)

Small succulent plants of the lily family, grown for their leaves which are usually thickened and tapering, often interestingly

HAWORTHIA MARGARITIFERA

marked, and arranged in a spreading or elongated rosette. Small white flowers on long stems may appear in the summer, but are not of particular significance. *H. margaritifera* forms a broad-based rosette about 15cm (6in) wide, with fleshy, dark green leaves. These taper to a sharp point and are attractively flecked with white.

Conditions Grow in a position with good light but out of direct sun, or in partial shade. Give warm temperatures in summer, cooler in winter, with a minimum of 4·5°C (40°F). Ventilation is not essential: haworthias grow well in ordinary home conditions.

Care Water plants to keep them moist during the summer. If winter conditions are cool, keep on the dry side; otherwise water sparingly.

Potting on Repot in late summer when necessary, using a well-drained compost such as equal parts John Innes No. 2 and coarse sand or grit.

Propagation From seed in spring, or from offsets, which are freely produced, in June. Detach these and dry them out for a couple of days before potting up individually.

Problems Given correct treatment, this plant is generally trouble-free. Stunted growth may indicate root mealy bug.

GYNURA SARMENTOSA

HEDERA CANARIENSIS 'VARIEGATA'

Canary Islands, North Africa
Canary Island Ivy
1m (3ft) or more

This is the hardy garden Ivy, with large, shallowly lobed leaves attractively marked green and silver-grey. *H. canariensis* is a bright, tall-growing plant ideal for cooler, slightly shaded areas. *H. helix* is generally slower-growing and well-suited to chilly dark places in the home. There are numerous varieties, with many different leaf shapes and colours through silver to dark green.

Conditions Grow *H. canariensis* in indirect light or a semi-shaded position. It does best in temperatures of about 13°C (55°F); temperatures over 16°C (60°F) will lead to problems. Once the plant is established it should be kept in the same position, as it dislikes change. It will survive the winter in an unheated room.

Care Keep compost moist in summer and water sparingly in winter. Never allow the compost to dry out. Mist frequently in summer, and in winter if grown in a heated room, and provide good ventilation. Train stems around canes; tie in all new growth and prevent aerial roots of mature plants attaching themselves to walls, as they may cling fast to decorated surfaces. Cut back and remove unwanted growth when necessary. Feed monthly with a liquid fertilizer from April to September.

Potting on When the roots fill the pot, normally annually, in March. Use John Innes No. 2 or a soil-less compost.

Problems Browning of leaf edges will occur in very hot rooms unless a plant is misted regularly. Red spider mite will attack in dry, poorly ventilated conditions. All forms will become spindly with too much light, but with too little the variegation may be affected. Restricted roots will also result in all-green leaves.

HEDERA CANARIENSIS 'VARIEGATA'

HELXINE SOLEIROLLII

HELXINE SOLEIROLII

**Corsica
Mind-your-own-business
Mat-forming**

A delightful and easy prostrate creeper, useful for ground cover and hanging baskets. The pink stems root as they grow, rapidly forming a neat mound of minute, pale green leaves. *H. soleirolii* may even be too easy at times – it will grow densely around the bases of taller plants and may smother other low-growing ones if left to grow on unchecked. *H. s.* 'Aurea' is the golden-leaved form.

Conditions A well-lit position without direct sun is ideal, but the plant will survive almost anywhere in a temperature between 7 and 24°C (45-75°F). Growing *H. soleirolii* with other plants helps to provide the humid atmosphere it prefers. Mist frequently.

Care Water freely in summer, more sparingly in winter, and avoid drowning the plant.

Potting on Usually treated as an annual and propagated each year, but can be potted on in April, in a loam-based compost, if large plants are wanted.

Propagation Detach rooted stem sections between April and September. Plantlets may be placed directly into their final growing position.

Problems Excess watering will cause stem and root rot. Underwatering causes browning of the foliage.

HEPTAPLEURUM ARBORICOLA

**Australasia
Parasol plant
60-90cm (2-3ft)**

A stately, tree-like plant, which may be grown equally effectively as a low shrubby plant if the growing tip is removed. Shiny, dark green leaflets are arranged in groups

HEPTAPLEURUM ARBORICOLA

of eight or ten, forming parasol-shaped leaves held out on long stalks from a central stem. *H. arboricola* is frequently labelled and sold as *Schefflera actinophylla*, which has a similar leaf form but much larger leaflets.

Conditions Grow in a well-lit position away from direct sun. Prefers a constant temperature of around 16°C (60°F), but will tolerate some fluctuation. Provide a slightly humid atmosphere by either growing with other plants or placing on a tray of moist pebbles.

Care Keep the soil evenly moist throughout the year. Mist the surrounding air frequently and sponge leaves occasionally with damp cotton wool. Give a liquid feed once a month during the growing season. Pinch out to shape when necessary.

Potting on Normally annually in spring, although only if the roots are filling the pot. Use a peat-based compost or John Innes No. 3.

Propagation Can be grown from leaf cuttings and seed, but this is difficult and is a task best left to specialist nurserymen.

Problems The more constant the conditions, the healthier the plant will be. Leaf fall may occur at any time if conditions are suddenly changed. Blackened leaf tips indicate overwatering.

HIPPEASTRUM

HIPPEASTRUM

South America
To 75cm (2½ft)

Popular winter-flowering bulbs with large and spectacular trumpet-shaped flowers on tall fleshy stems; related to and commonly sold as amaryllis. The strap-shaped, arching, mid-green leaves continue to develop after the flowers have died back. Hippeastrum can be grown in succession to flower most of the year in colours ranging from white to pinks and bright reds. Bulbs can be bought on their own, or potted up and ready to flower.

Conditions When in bud, place in bright light away from direct sun, at a temperature of around 18°C (65°F).

Care and cultivation of bulb Soak the lower part of the bulb in tepid water for four to five days, then pot in 12·5-18cm (5-7in) pots in a mixture of loam, leaf mould and sand, or John Innes No. 2 potting compost, leaving half the bulb exposed. Hippeastrums flourish with good bottom heat – an ideal position is on a shelf over a radiator. Water sparingly at first and in-

crease watering when the buds appear, and place in good light for development and flowering. The flowering period will be lengthened if plants are moved to a cooler position once the flower heads have appeared. Water cautiously from the top; too much water will rot the bulb. Mist the leaves occasionally.

Care after flowering Do not cut the flower stems back until they have completely dried out. Place the plant in a sunny, well-ventilated position, continue to water sparingly and give a fortnightly liquid feed. A plant which has flowered in early summer should be rested in early autumn, and watering should cease by October. The cycle will restart after six weeks.

Potting on and propagation Pot on every two years. Offsets develop around large bulbs, and they can be separated from the parent bulb at repotting time and potted up individually.

Problems Generally trouble-free.

See also *Bulbs*, page 25-27.

HOWEA FORSTERIANA

HOWEA FORSTERIANA

Lord Howe Islands
Kentia palm
To 4m (12ft)

A beautiful and elegant specimen plant, and the most frequently seen of the tall palms, with an upright growth habit and long graceful fronds which arch outwards in maturity. It is slow growing, and unless bought as a mature specimen it will take many years to reach its full height as a pot-grown plant.

Conditions Grow in a position of semi-shade, or light shade out of direct sun. Give warm temperatures in summer and a minimum of 13°C (55°F) in winter, with some additional humidity if the air is very hot and dry. Give some ventilation in summer, but avoid draughts.

Care Water liberally in summer, using rain or softened water, and sparingly in winter; drain thoroughly. Take care never to let plants become waterlogged or left standing in water, as the base and roots are easily rotted. Mist plants regularly and sponge the leaves occasionally with plain water. Give occasional weak liquid feeds during the growing season. Cut off any lower fronds that have died back.

Potting on In spring, and only when plants are pot-bound and the root ball is pushing out of the pot. Pot on until a final pot size of 20-25cm (8-10in) is reached; thereafter top-dress each year in spring. Use a peat-based compost (John Innes No. 3) with added sand for drainage, and line pots with broken crocks to improve drainage even further. Pack the soil firmly around the root ball.

Propagation From seed, at a temperature of 27°C (80°F).

Problems Brown tips on the leaves may be caused by underwatering in summer, or by dry air. Brown spots on the leaves can be the result of overwatering or the use of

HOYA BELLA
Hoya carnosa (not illustrated) is similar but larger

hard tap water. Brown and falling leaves may be the natural death of lower leaves, or, if combined with signs of rotting at the base of the stem, may be due to over-watering or poor drainage.

HOYA BELLA

India
22-30cm (9-12in)

A shrubby shape combined with its arching habit makes this plant a good choice for a hanging basket or a pedestal. The fleshy oval leaves are light green, sometimes with silver markings. Clusters of waxy, star-shaped flowers, white with rose or purple centres, appear sporadically between spring and autumn.

Conditions Grow in a lightly shaded position. Give warmth in summer and a minimum temperature of 10°C (50°F) in winter; bring up to temperatures of 16°C (60°F) and over as the flowers are opening. *H. bella* needs the same humid conditions as

H. carnosa, but is generally a much more difficult plant; it needs higher temperatures, but must not be placed in direct sun.

Care Water freely in summer and sparingly in winter, allowing compost to dry out in between waterings. Give a liquid feed every two to three weeks during the growing period. Never move the plant once buds have formed, and do not remove dead flower heads or mist the plant when in bloom. Pinch out the growing tips of young plants.

Potting on Necessary only when the plant is completely pot-bound. Use a soil-less compost or John Innes No. 2. Spring or early summer is the ideal time. It will grow and flower in a 12·5cm (5in) pot but is best in a 25cm (10in) hanging basket.

Propagation Take 7·5-10cm (3-4in) stem cuttings from young growth in summer.

Problems Generally trouble-free, but over-watering will result in the leaves turning brown.

HOYA CARNOSA

**Queensland
Wax plant
To 5m (16ft)**

A rampant climber with strongly scented, waxy, white, star-shaped flowers hanging in clusters from short stalks and appearing from May to September. The plant has the curious habit of forming the whole stem of its new growth before any leaves develop. There are two variegated forms, one with pink margins which fade to cream, the other with gold centres and dark green margins; both make excellent foliage plants, the flowers being an added bonus when they appear on two-year-old specimens.

Conditions Position in bright light in a well-ventilated area, avoiding direct sun and draughts. Grow in constant average temperatures with a winter minimum of 10°C (50°F), but increase this to 16-18°C (60-65°F) as the flower buds start to open. Maintain a humid atmosphere throughout spring and summer, and keep pots standing on damp pebbles or in moistened peat. *Hoya carnosa* adheres by means of aerial shoots, and a damp sphagnum moss stick should be provided.

Care Water freely in summer, and keep the plant on the dry side in winter. Mist the leaves in hot weather, but not during flowering periods. Feed every three weeks during the growing period with a liquid fertilizer. Avoid moving the plant once the flower buds have begun to form, and do not remove dead flower heads. Pinch out the growing tips of young plants; overgrown plants may be cut back, but are slow to recover and are better replaced.

Potting on Examine the root ball annually and pot on only when the plant is potbound, using a soil-less compost or John Innes No. 2.

Propagation From 7·5-10cm (3-4in) cuttings of mature growth, during the summer.

HYDRANGEA MACROPHYLLA

Problems Check regularly for mealy bug, which often inhabits areas between the stems and their support. Scale insects may also be a problem. Yellowing leaves are an indication of overwatering.

HYDRANGEA MACROPHYLLA

China, Japan
To 60cm (2ft)

This well-known flowering garden shrub makes a splendid indoor 'feature' plant. The large rounded heads are composed of clusters of white, pink, or blue flowers which bloom for six weeks or more during spring and early summer. They are set amongst mid-green oval leaves.

Conditions Provide a semi-shaded, well-ventilated position. Cool conditions are vital for prolonged flowering; maintain temperatures of between 7 and 16°C (45-60°F). In hard water areas, to preserve the colour of blue-flowered forms it is essential to maintain acidity in the soil by using only rainwater. They will already have been chemically treated by the grower with a blueing powder (alum) which increases soil acidity.

Care Water freely throughout the growing season. After flowering, remove the dead blooms by cutting back the stem to two leaf shoots below the flower. Pot-grown plants are seldom kept for a second season, but by reducing all growth to two good pairs of leaves, and overwintering the plant either outside in a cold frame or in a very cold room indoors, it is possible to bring it back into flower for a second year. Water sparingly during this period, and in January bring the plant in to warmer conditions and increase watering.

Potting on At the end of summer when plants are cut back. Young plants should be potted on annually. Ensure good drainage by placing a layer of crocks at the base of the pot, and leave sufficient room at the top for ample watering. Use a lime-free loam-based compost (John Innes No. 3).

HYPOESTES SANGUINOLENTA

Propagation Take cuttings from blind (non-flowering) shoots in late summer.

Problems Alkaline soil causes chlorosis, which shows as yellowing between the veins, or as leaves that are almost white.

HYPOESTES SANGUINOLENTA

Madagascar
Polka dot plant
To 45cm (1½ft)

An attractive and delicate low-growing plant, with small, oval, olive-green leaves covered with tiny pinkish-white spots. Uninteresting mauve and white flowers appear during the summer.

Conditions Grow in a well-ventilated and bright position away from direct sun to encourage good colour variation. Give a warm position, with a minimum winter temperature of 13°C (55°F). Maintain a humid atmosphere during the summer, and plunge the pot in moistened peat or stand it on wet pebbles.

Care Keep compost evenly moist. Water regularly from spring to autumn with tepid rainwater, and mist frequently. Pinch out growing tips regularly to prevent stems becoming straggly.

Potting on and propagation Plants are normally discarded at the end of the growing season, but may be overwintered and repotted the following spring. Hypoestes can be grown easily from seed in spring, and are not normally worth overwintering since they require constant warmth and invariably become straggly. However, the quality of colours in each seed batch varies considerably and it may be worth preserving a good coloured plant, to be propagated from young tip cuttings in spring.

IMPATIENS

IMPATIENS

Africa
Busy Lizzie
30-60cm (1-2ft)

A group of popular, free-flowering, bushy plants with fleshy stems and attractive, pointed oval leaves. The spurred, simple-petalled flowers are borne in profusion in shades of red, salmon, cream and white, and there are some 'candystriped' forms. Nearly all are hybrids or cultivars of *I. holstii* (syn. *I. wallerana*) and *I. sultanii*. The New Guinea hybrids often have particularly attractive variegated leaves, and although they flower less profusely and need a slightly higher temperature, they are well worth growing.

Conditions In summer grow in bright light, shaded from direct sun, and give some ventilation; a windowsill is ideal as long as it does not face south. Temperatures should be average, with a winter minimum of 13°C (55°F). The New Guinea hybrids need somewhat warmer and more humid conditions; grow in a minimum winter temperature of 18°C (65°F), and sink pots in moistened peat.

Care Water freely in summer; keep compost moist at all times. Reduce watering in winter if the plant is not flowering, but never let the compost dry out. All varieties will benefit from a regular misting during warm weather, but avoid wetting the open blooms. Give a fortnightly liquid feed from April to September.

Pruning Essential for bushy growth; pinch out growing tips regularly. Leggy plants can be cut back to encourage shoot growth at the base. Prune mature plants each spring.

Potting on Plants will flower freely only when pot-bound. Pot on when absolutely necessary in spring, using John Innes No. 2 or a soil-less compost.

Propagation From seed sown in spring or from stem cuttings, which root easily in water. Water very cautiously at first and spray leaves frequently. Water normally when roots are established.

Problems Wilting, falling leaves are the result of lack of water. Rotting stems are the consequence of overwatering; never allow the plants to stand in water. Spindly growth is caused by too much warmth and inadequate light; plants naturally become leggy with age – take cuttings and discard. Poor flowering is caused by over-potting. Loss of flowers is normally due to lack of light, but dry air, underwatering or attack by red spider mite will have the same effect if growing conditions are poor.

JASMINUM POLYANTHUM

JASMINUM POLYANTHUM

China
Jasmine
To 3m (10ft)

A graceful flowering climber with fragrant, white to almost pink, star-shaped flowers growing in panicles from slender twining stems between winter and spring. The delicate pinnate leaves with many leaflets in opposite pairs arch slightly away from the stems. It is a rampant grower and needs to be cut back regularly.

Conditions Grow in good light with some direct sun in winter for early flowering. Give average to warm summer temperatures, and around 7°C (45°F) in winter. Plants can be brought into flower earlier by increasing winter temperatures, but this will also encourage rapid growth. If space is limited, growth can be controlled by planting in relatively small pots. Provide a humid atmosphere by sinking pots in damp peat or setting on moist pebbles. Train the plant on canes or wires, and provide some fresh air during the summer; a plant that can be moved without too much difficulty will benefit from a spell outside.

Care Compost should be kept moist at all times. Water frequently in summer but sparingly in winter – too much watering will damage roots and affect flowering. Mist regularly.

Pruning Pinch out growing tips regularly to encourage development of side shoots, and cut back all shoots after flowering in late spring or early summer.

Potting on When necessary in spring, in John Innes No. 2 potting compost.

Propagation Cuttings taken with a heel in spring will root very easily. Jasmine can also be propagated by layering in late summer.

Problems Troubles are minimal, although aphids and mealy bugs may attack young shoots.

KALANCHOË BLOSSFELDIANA 'VULCAN'

KALANCHOË BLOSSFELDIANA 'VULCAN'

Madagascar
15-25cm (6-10in)

This is the well-known Christmas-flowering succulent, which flowers naturally from February, but is brought into flower earlier by reducing its exposure to daylight. It is a shrubby plant with rounded, slightly serrated, fleshy leaves which turn slightly red when exposed to sunlight. Clusters of small red tubular flowers are borne on leafless stems which grow above the foliage. Other hybrids have yellow or orange blooms.

Conditions Will grow well on a sunny window ledge but should be moved to a shadier position for a resting period of about a month after flowering. Give average to warm summer temperatures and a winter minimum of 7°C (45°F).

Care Water thoroughly throughout the summer, but allow the surface of the compost to dry out before rewatering. Water sparingly in winter, keeping the compost just moist during the resting period. Reduce the height of the plant by one-third after flowering.

Potting on and propagation Pot on in spring, after the annual resting period is over, using John Innes No. 2 or a soil-less compost. However, plants tend to become uncontrollably straggly after one year and are often better discarded. Good stock can easily be continued by 7·5-10cm (3-4in) cuttings taken between May and September. Allow them to dry for two days before potting up into the plant's usual growing medium.

Problems May be attacked by mealy bug.

See also *Cacti and Succulents*, page 21-22.

LILIUM LONGIFLORUM

LILIUM LONGIFLORUM

Japan
Easter lily
To 1m (3ft)

A heavily fragrant member of the lily family, which, in spite of its name, actually blooms in July and August, though it may be forced into bloom earlier. Many large, trumpet-shaped flowers, white with golden pollen, are borne on long single stems.

Conditions To cultivate bulbs, pot them in autumn and keep in a cool dark place to encourage top growth. Pot well down in the compost, leaving room for the roots which grow at the base of the stems. When top growth appears, gradually bring into the light in slightly warmer conditions, but avoid direct sun. Lilies thrive with cool night-time temperatures which should never exceed 10°C (50°F).

Care Keep compost moist at all times during the growing period. Reduce watering after flowering as the leaves begin to die away, but do not allow the compost to dry out completely. Increase watering again at the start of the next growing season.

Potting on In autumn, in 15cm (6in) pots of John Innes No. 1 potting compost. Provide good drainage by placing a layer of crocks in the base of the pot.

Propagation From bulbils which grow on the stem just below ground level. Detach in early autumn and pot up separately; they will reach flowering size after three years.

See also *Bulbs*, page 25-27.

MAMMILLARIA BOCASANA

Mexico
15cm (6in)

One of a large number of attractive, small-growing, cylindrical or globular cacti, with prominent spines or tubercles arranged in spiral rings around the body. Long-lasting flowers appear in a garland around the top of the stem in spring and summer and are sometimes succeeded by brightly coloured fruits. *M. bocasana* is one of the easiest mammillarias to grow and bring into flower in the home. The blue-green cylindrical stem is covered in white, hooked spines and hairs, and cream-yellow flowers are borne in the spring, followed by rose-pink seed pods. New stems are produced around the base to form a cluster.

Conditions Position in good light with plenty of sun, and turn regularly to ensure that growth is even. Temperatures should be warm in summer and cool in winter – 4·5-7°C (40-45°F). No humidity is required.

Care Water thoroughly in summer, allowing the soil to become touch-dry between waterings. Withhold water in winter unless the plant is kept in warm conditions, when it will require only enough to prevent it from shrivelling. Give fortnightly liquid feeds with a high-potassium fertilizer in the growing season.

Potting on Repot into the next pot size annually in spring, or when necessary, using a rich mixture such as John Innes No. 2 with added sand for drainage. Bone meal

MAMMILLARIA BOCASANA

coloured with red veins and a yellow midrib on a dark green background. *M. l. kerchoveana*, another fine variety, has pale green leaves with dark brown blotches running either side of the veins, and may grow to 30cm (12in) across.

Conditions Grow in a shaded position from April to September – the coloured leaves fade quickly in strong light. Provide a constantly warm humid atmosphere and avoid extremes of temperature between day and night. The minimum winter temperature should be 13°C (55°F); plants will deteriorate rapidly in a lower temperature. Plunge pots in containers filled with moist peat and keep well away from draughts. Marantas grow well with other plants in a terrarium or a tropical plant window.

Care Water freely from March to September but sparingly during winter. Use tepid rainwater if possible. Mist daily during

warm weather and give a liquid feed fortnightly during the growing season.

Potting on Marantas grow rapidly during their early years and should be potted on regularly to a final pot size of 15cm (6in). Top-dress mature plants annually, using peat-based compost.

Propagation The plants grow from rhizomes which can be divided and replanted in April. Keep new plants covered with polythene in a warm place until the roots are established.

Problems Curled or discoloured leaves are the result of overexposure to bright light. Brown dry leaf tips, leaf fall and poor growth indicate dry air, which may encourage red spider mite. Dry, yellowing leaves followed by leaf fall is due to inadequate watering. Limp and rotten stems are the result of overwatering in winter.

may be added to the compost in spring or when repotting.

Propagation From seed in spring, or from offsets detached and potted up individually into the usual growing compost.

Problems Generally trouble-free if given correct treatment. Discoloration of the top of the plant or collapse of the stem may occur if the plant is incorrectly watered.

See also *Cacti and Succulents*, page 21-22.

MARANTA LEUCONEURA ERYTHROPHYLLA

Brazil
Prayer plant
15-20cm (6-8in)

The marantas are a group of beautiful foliage plants which all have the curious habit of closing their leaves together and holding them upright in the evening, a habit which explains the common name of prayer plant. *M. l. erythrophylla* is of rather erect habit, with oval velvety leaves which are richly

MARANTA LEUCONEURA ERYTHROPHYLLA

MONSTERA DELICIOSA

MONSTERA DELICIOSA

Mexico
Swiss cheese plant
To 2·4m (8ft) or more

A large feature plant with leathery, glossy, rich green leaves which develop holes and slashed edges as they mature. Young leaves are heart-shaped and complete. The plant typically develops aerial roots, and although it will not achieve the stature reached in its natural habitat, given suitable conditions it will quite rapidly grow to 2·4m (8ft) and develop leaves of over 65cm (2ft) in width. Monsteras also produce creamy-white, lily-like flowers and edible fruits, but in normal domestic conditions it is highly unlikely that either will appear

Conditions Grow in a lightly shaded position. Give moderate temperatures – active growth starts at 18°C (65°F) – and a minimum of 10°C (50°F) in winter. Support is necessary and is best provided by a permanently moist sphagnum moss stick into which the aerial shoots can grow; it will also provide some humidity.

Care Water thoroughly during the growing season, but allow the compost to dry out slightly between waterings. Waterlogging will cause rotting of the roots. Water sparingly from November to March. Mist the leaves and clean them regularly with a moist sponge. Encourage aerial roots to grow into the compost or, as the plant matures, into the moss stick. Give fortnightly liquid feeds from April to September.

Potting on Will probably be necessary annually until a 30cm (12in) pot size is reached, after which the plant should be top-dressed annually. Use a peat-based compost with extra coarse sand added.

Propagation Remove the growing tip with one mature leaf in June, and place in equal parts peat and sand at a temperature of 24-27°C (75-80°F). Between June and August, if several new plants are wanted and the parent plant needs to be reduced in height, remove the top part of the stem and cut into 7·4cm (3in) long sections, each with a leaf. Root as for tip cuttings.

Problems Usually a result of incorrect treatment. Rotting stems may occur in winter when fungae are encouraged by too much moisture and lack of heat; the plant may be saved by repotting. In dry conditions red spider mite may attack. Lack of holes and incisions in mature leaves may be due to lack of light, cold air, too little water or underfeeding. On taller plants it is probably caused by water failing to reach the top of the plant. Ensure aerial roots are kept moist; if necessary pack them with sphagnum moss fastened with twine. Brown or yellow patches, brown and papery tips and edges, leggy growth and small leaves indicate too little moisture or too little light.

NEPHROLEPIS EXALTATA 'BOSTONIENSIS'

Tropics
Boston fern
45-60cm (1½-2ft)

This very popular fern has lovely, wide-spreading, rather frilly fronds, and is seen at its best in a hanging basket. *N. exaltata* is a fast-growing fern with many cultivars which will grow well in centrally-heated rooms provided they are given some humidity. The plants throw out runners from the tops of their rhizomes.

Conditions Grow in a draught-free position with good indirect light. Maintain constant temperatures of between 16 and

21°C (60-70°F), with a winter minimum of 10°C (50°F). In warm temperatures provide a constantly humid atmosphere by misting daily around the plant. Take care not to wet the fronds themselves too much, as they are easily damaged. Avoid exposure to fumes and keep away from sources of direct heat.

Care Keep the compost evenly moist all year round, but water less frequently in winter if conditions are cooler. Never over-water. Give a fortnightly liquid feed during the growing season.

Potting on In spring, when roots fill the pot. Young plants will need to be potted on annually in a well-drained compost. Use equal quantities of John Innes No. 2 potting compost and peat, or 1 part moss peat, 1 part peat-based compost and 1 part sharp sand.

Propagation Divide the rhizomes, making sure each section has some roots and fronds, or pin the young plantlets which form at the ends of the runners into compost.

Problems The commonest cause of trouble is incorrect treatment. Yellowing, shrivel-led fronds and dying back are caused by a hot dry atmosphere or dry compost. Limp, wilting, yellowing fronds are the result of overwatering.

PELARGONIUM CRISPUM

PELARGONIUM CRISPUM

South Africa
Scented-leaved geranium
60cm (2ft) or more

Unlike the other pelargonium groups, the scented-leaved pelargoniums are grown for their various and distinctive scents and interesting foliage, rather than their rather insignificant flowers. *P. crispum* is a lemon balm-scented variety, with slender, up-right, branching stems and mid-green, fan-shaped leaves; the variegated form has creamy-white margins. Small clusters of pink flowers appear from May to October. *P. graveolens*, with a rose scent and spread-ing habit, has grey-green, palmate leaves which are very deeply lobed and toothed. Rose-pink flowers, arranged in umbels, appear in June and July. *P. tomentosum* is a peppermint-scented variety with rather beautiful, pale green, velvety leaves and very long, lax, hairy stems which can be trained into a fan shape.

Conditions Grow in a bright position but protect from midday sun. The scent is re-leased when the plants are touched, so keep them in a position where their leaves will by brushed by passers-by.

Otherwise treat as *P. hortorum*.

NEPHROLEPIS EXALTATA 'BOSTONIENSIS'

PELARGONIUM DOMESTICUM

PELARGONIUM DOMESTICUM (REGALE)

South Africa
Regal geranium
37-60cm (15-24in)

Large, showy, frilled flowers, up to 5cm (2in) wide, grow in umbels during April and May. Some modern varieties have longer flowering periods. The flowers, which are usually blotched or veined with a darker colour, are available in subtle shades, including a delicate pink and a dark maroon-purple. The mid-green leaves are roughly triangular with finely serrated edges.

Conditions Provide the same conditions as for *P. hortorum*, but with the higher winter temperature of 10°C (50°F).

Care As for *P. hortorum*, but plants should be cut back less drastically, in the autumn.

Potting on As for *P. hortorum*.

Propagation As for *P. hortorum*.

Problems As for *P. hortorum. P domesticum* is more susceptible to attack by pests. If the plant is not flowering, but is generally healthy, the most probable cause is overheating.

PELARGONIUM HORTORUM

South Africa
Geranium
60-90cm (2-3ft)

The free-flowering zonal varieties form the largest group of pelargoniums and are commonly referred to as 'geraniums'. They are easily distinguished by their rounded, slightly crinkled leaves, which have a contrasting horseshoe mark or 'zone' around them. The dense round umbels of single or double flowers in white, pinks or reds, appear from late spring to autumn. *P. peltatum* is a trailing variety that is ideal for hanging baskets; it has ivy-shaped leaves and large single or double blooms which are freely borne from summer to autumn.

Conditions Grow in a well-lit position with as much direct sun as possible. The plants do well in average warmth with cool nights and a minimum winter temperature of 7°C (45°F). *P. peltatum* prefers a slightly higher winter temperature of 10°C (50°F). Give as much ventilation as possible during the summer.

Care Water plants thoroughly, then allow the compost to become moderately dry before rewatering. Pelargoniums have semi-succulent stems and can survive periods of drought, but will not tolerate waterlogged roots. Water sparingly in winter; the compost should be just moist when the plant is not flowering. Give a fortnightly liquid feed during the growing season. Remove dead flowers regularly, and never mist.

Pruning Cut back hard in spring, to force side shoots – this is essential for bushy growth.

Potting on When absolutely necessary in spring, in John Innes No. 2 potting compost.

Propagation From 5cm (2in) stem cuttings in late August and early September. Allow cuttings to dry out for 24 hours before placing in equal quantities of sand and peat. Keep away from direct sun and do not cover. Cuttings may be taken in March but tend to produce smaller flowers.

Problems Usually the result of incorrect treatment. Blackening of the stem base is caused by black leg disease: destroy the infected plant and in future always use a sterile compost and avoid overwatering. Oedema disease is seen as corky scabs on the undersides of the leaves: reduce watering. Grey mould on leaves is botrytis; remove damaged leaves, reduce watering and increase ventilation. Reddening of the leaves is due to low temperatures – keep plants away from windows on frosty nights. Yellowing of firm leaves and scorched edges indicates underwatering. Leaves wilting and rotten indicates overwatering. Too little light will result in spindly growth.

PELLAEA ROTUNDIFOLIA

New Zealand
Button fern
To 45cm (1½ft) in length

A charming spreading fern with small rounded leaves, ideal for ground cover in plant arrangements, where it will tolerate most conditions and benefit from the humidity created by surrounding plants. It grows equally well hanging over the side of a small pot. *P. rotundifolia* is one of the easiest ferns to grow in drier conditions.

Conditions Grow in good indirect light or in semi shade. Give warm to moderate temperatures, with a minimum of 10°C (50°F) in winter. Mist around plants occasionally.

Care Keep compost moist and water more sparingly in winter. Give a weak liquid feed once a fortnight during the growing season.

Potting on In spring, when roots fill the pot; use a peat-based compost.

Propagation In spring, by division of rhizomes when repotting, or from spores.

Problems Generally trouble-free.

PELARGONIUM HORTORUM

PELLAEA ROTUNDIFOLIA

PEPEROMIA CAPERATA

ber; plunge pots in moistened peat or rest on damp pebbles, and mist twice a day during hot weather. In winter ensure that there is some ventilation, but avoid draughts. The plants thrive under fluorescent light and make ideal specimens for bottle gardens and terrariums.

Care Water sparingly at all times. Allow the compost to dry out between waterings, and keep almost dry throughout the winter. Water from beneath, or carefully from above – the stems rot very easily – and use tepid water. Give occasional liquid feeds from May to September.

Potting on Normally annually in April, but the maximum pot size necessary is 9cm (3½in). Peperomias have very small root systems and are virtually epiphytic in the jungles of South America, which are their natural habitat. Use a peat-based soil-less compost or John Innes No. 1.

Propagation By division in spring. *P. caperata* can also be increased by leaf cuttings.

Problems Grey mould (botrytis) will appear at the base of stems if the air is too stagnant. Brown-tipped leaves may be caused by sudden drops in temperature. Remove the leaves immediately and always keep the plants away from draughts and cold window-sills. Overwatering will result in wilting or discoloured leaves and/or stem and leaf rot.

PEPEROMIA CAPERATA

South America
10-25cm (4-10in)

A dainty, compact plant with dark green, heart-shaped, corrugated leaves which have purple markings running along the ridges. Curiously crooked white flower spikes with pinkish-red stems grow erect above the foliage from April to December. *P. caperata* makes a perfect foil for the larger variegated peperomias. *P. sandersii* has silver bands running along its smooth dark green leaves, which grow up to 10cm (4in) long. *P. marmorata* is similar but its leaves are bluish-green with darker veins. Other good species include *P. hederaefolia*, which is similar in most respects to *P. caperata* but has slightly larger leaves, and *P. obtusifolia* which grows to about 30cm (12in) and usually has red-edged leaves, although there is also a variety with cream-edged leaves.

Conditions Grow in good light. A slightly shaded position away from direct sun is ideal during the summer months, but in winter give it as much light as possible. Give average temperatures, with a winter minimum of 10°C (50°F) for *P. caperata* and 13°C (55°F) for *P. sandersii*. Provide a humid atmosphere from April to Septem-

PEPEROMIA MAGNOLIAEFOLIA 'VARIEGATA'

San Domingo
Desert privet
20cm (8in)

A freely branching species of peperomia with an upright spreading shape and glossy, slightly fleshy, oval leaves, white at first but becoming variegated as they mature. The climbing or trailing *P. scandens* 'Variegata' has the same fleshy leaves, but these are heart-shaped and have a pale cream colouring which becomes pale green with cream margins. *P. scandens* is difficult in

PEPEROMIA MAGNOLIAEFOLIA

effective when suspended in a large basket from a high ceiling.

Conditions Grow in a lightly shaded area, just out of direct sun. It thrives in warm conditions, with a minimum winter temperature of 13°C (55°F) and with high humidity. The pot can be plunged in permanently moist peat, but, unlike other philodendrons, _P. bipinnatifidum_ will tolerate less than perfect conditions.

Care Water thoroughly from April to October, but allow the compost to dry out slightly between waterings. Water sparingly during the winter months; overwatering at any time may result in root rot. Mist the leaves frequently, and give a liquid feed once a fortnight during the growing season. Wipe the leaves regularly with a moist sponge.

Potting on For young plants, normally every two years, when roots fill the pot. Top-dress mature plants annually. Use a peat-based compost and place some crocks at the bottom to help balance the plant and improve drainage.

Propagation By seed, but difficult.

Problems Usually due to incorrect watering. Lack of incisions in mature leaves may be a result of poor light, cold air, insufficient water or underfeeding. On tall specimens it may be due to the failure of water to reach the upper leaves: make sure the aerial roots receive adequate moisture, packing them if necessary with sphagnum moss fastened with twine. Overwatering in winter may cause rotting of the stems. In dry conditions red spider mite may be a problem.

its early stages, when exposure to excessive damp during cold periods can result in severe leaf drop, but is easier to maintain once established.

Conditions Give the same conditions as for _P. caperata_, but _P. scandens_ benefits from a higher winter temperature of 16°C (60°F).

Care As for _P. caperata_. Avoid using cold water in winter. The growing tips of _P. magnoliaefolia_ 'Variegata' should be pinched out at the start of the growing season to encourage its bushy habit.

Problems As for _P. caperata_.

PHILODENDRON BIPINNATIFIDUM

Brazil
Tree philodendron
To 1m (3ft)

A low-growing plant and one of the most handsome members of the philodendron group. Dark shiny green, deeply incised leaves, up to 50cm (20in) across, are held out on long, stiff, fleshy stems. The immature leaves which are produced for the first two years of growth are heart-shaped. A splendid specimen plant, it looks equally

PHILODENDRON BIPINNATIFIDUM

PHILODENDRON HASTATUM

PHILODENDRON HASTATUM

Brazil
Elephant's ear
1·5m (5ft)

The elephant's ear philodendron has mid-green, arrow-shaped, very glossy leaves which grow to 18cm (7in) in length, and are carried on broad, fleshy leaf stalks. This is a moderately vigorous climbing variety which should be grown up a sphagnum moss stick to provide anchorage for the aerial roots and support for the stem.

Conditions Keep in a lightly shaded spot with moderate brightness, but no direct sun. Give moderate summer temperatures and a minimum of 10°C (50°F) in winter, though 13°C (55°F) is better. Provide a humid atmosphere by placing the pot on damp pebbles or sinking it in a container filled with damp peat.

Care Water thoroughly from April to October, allowing the compost to dry slightly in between waterings. Overwatering can cause root rot. Water sparingly during the winter. Give a fortnightly liquid feed from April to October. Mist frequently, and clean the leaves.

Potting on Normally necessary every other year, but once a 20cm (10in) pot has been reached, mature plants should be given a top-dressing every year. Use a peat-based compost.

Propagation From tip cuttings in May or June in a close atmosphere. Take 12·5-15cm (4-6in) sections, each with a mature leaf. Place in 7·5cm (3in) pots of peat and place in an open propagator, or cover and provide some bottom heat. Stem cuttings with joints, taken in May or June, will root under the same conditions.

Problems Generally trouble-free, but over-watering will result in yellowing of leaves and premature leaf fall. Red spider mite will attack if the air is too dry.

PHILODENDRON SCANDENS

Panama
Sweetheart plant
2m (6ft) or more

A strong evergreen climber with slender stems and bright, mid-green, heart-shaped leaves with narrow tapering points. This is a tolerant species which, like most climbing members of the philodendron group, produces aerial shoots.

Conditions Position away from direct sun; it will grow in shady areas but benefits from periods of indirect light. Give average tem-

PHILODENDRON SCANDENS

peratures, not less than 10°C (50°F) in winter. It tolerates dry air but prefers a slightly humid atmosphere. *P. scandens* will trail, but is happier when grown up a sphagnum moss stick, where its aerial roots may be pressed into the compost and provide moisture for its upper leaves.

Care Water thoroughly from April to October, but sparingly in winter. Give a liquid feed every two weeks from May to September. Keep the moss stick moist and pinch out the growing tips frequently to encourage the growth of side shoots.

Potting on Usually every two years. Pot on when the roots have filled the pot, using John Innes No. 2 or a peat-based compost.

Propagation Take tip cuttings, 10-15cm (4-6in) long with one mature leaf in May or June. Use 7·5cm (3in) pots filled with equal quantities of sand and peat, and provide some bottom heat. Stem cuttings taken with a joint will also root easily.

Problems Usually due to incorrect treatment – too little water in summer, too much water in winter. Weak leggy growth may be due to insufficient light, or may indicate that the plant needs repotting.

PHOENIX CANARIENSIS

Canary Islands
2·4-3m (8-10ft)

A relative of the date palm, *P. canariensis* makes a charming indoor palm with slender, stiff, slightly arching fronds. It is very slow growing and unlikely to attain its full height for many years, but in any case is most attractive as a young plant. In its natural habitat it is smaller than the date palm, but produces similar fruits.

Conditions Grow in a brightly lit, airy position with shading from the brightest sun. Temperatures should be cool, with a minimum of 7°C (45°F) in winter. Keep well ventilated in warm weather and in summer place outside in light shade if possible.

Care Water freely in summer but sparingly in winter, using tepid softened water and keeping well drained. Mist around the plants occasionally if the atmosphere becomes hot and dry. Give a fortnightly liquid feed from May to September.

Potting on Every second or third year, in spring, or when necessary. Pot on to a final pot size of 25-30cm (10-12in), then top-dress every other year in spring. Line pots with broken crocks to ensure efficient drainage, and use a well-drained loam-based growing medium such as John Innes No. 2 potting compost.

Propagation From seed, in spring.

Problems Usually a result of incorrect treatment. Keep plants in cool airy conditions, and never allow them to become waterlogged.

See also *Palms*, page 23-24.

PHOENIX CANARIENSIS

PILEA CADIEREI

PILEA CADIEREI

Vietnam
Aluminium plant
30cm (1ft)

A striking foliage plant with an upright bushy habit. The form 'Nana' is the most common. The dark green, oval leaves have silvery blotches in between the veins, giving the plant a metallic sheen.

Conditions Grow in a well-ventilated, light or semi-shaded position. Avoid direct sun during the summer, but give full light during the winter to encourage the unusual variegation. Temperatures should be moderate to warm in the summer, with a winter minimum of 10°C (50°F). Maintain a humid atmosphere, particularly at the start of the growing season, by keeping pots standing on wet pebbles. Never leave on windowsills on frosty nights, and avoid draughts.

Care Water liberally with tepid water from spring through to autumn, and more sparingly in winter. Give fortnightly liquid feeds from June to September. In spring pinch out the growing tips to encourage the growth of side shoots and a full shape.

Potting on When the roots fill the pot, probably annually. Use a loam-based compost or John Innes No. 2.

Propagation Plants become leggy after three to four years and are better discarded. They are easily replaced from stem cuttings taken in May; pot in equal proportions of sand and peat and root at a temperature of 18-21°C (65-70°F).

Problems Excessive leaf fall in winter indicates either overwatering or low temperatures. Some leaf fall is quite normal. Discoloured leaves with brown tips and edges are caused by overexposure to light or to a sudden drop in temperature.

PILEA NUMMULARIFOLIA

South America
Creeping Charlie
Mat-forming

This is a dainty, low-growing creeper, ideal for trailing over hanging baskets. Tiny, yellowish-green, rounded leaves with corrugated surfaces trail on wiry, reddish stems which throw out roots as they grow.

Conditions Grow in a well-ventilated and light position away from direct sun. Pileas will grow in shade, but will tend to produce leggy growth. Give warmth, with a minimum temperature of 10°C (50°F) in

PILEA NUMMULARIFOLIA

winter, and a humid atmosphere. Stand pots in containers of moist peat and keep well away from draughts.

Care Water liberally with tepid water from spring to autumn, but allow the compost to dry slightly in between waterings. Reduce watering in winter and allow the compost to remain dry for rather longer. Spray occasionally with tepid water and give liquid feeds fortnightly during the summer.

Potting on Usually necessary every spring; use John Innes No. 2 potting compost.

Propagation Detach and pot up rooted stems. Plants are best renewed every two years.

Problems Heavy leaf fall is the result of cold wet compost, but even healthy plants will shed a few leaves in winter. Discoloured leaves with brown tips and edges are a result either of too much shade or of a sudden drop in temperature.

PLATYCERIUM BIFURCATUM

Australia
Stag's horn fern
45-75cm (1½-2½ft)

A strange but striking-looking epiphytic fern which grows on the branches of forest trees in its natural habitat. It bears two types of frond, each quite distinct from the other. Broad, ribbon-like, fertile fronds project from the centre of the plant, forming long 'antlers'. These are dark green but have a covering of very fine white hairs which give them a velvety-grey appearance. The spores are borne on the underside of their tips. Underneath are the broad, fan-shaped sterile fronds, which grow in layers, the lower ones slowly dying off to provide food for the roots. These provide a natural anchor for the plant.

Conditions *P. bifurcatum* may be either attached with wire and grown on moss-covered bark or cork, or grown in moss-filled baskets. Keep in a well-lit position away from direct sun. Give warmth, with a minimum winter temperature of 10°C (50°F), and maintain a humid atmosphere. Mist the plant frequently.

Care Immerse the basket or bark in soft tepid water once a week during the summer and allow to drain before rehanging. Reduce the frequency of watering in winter, keeping the compost just moist. Never remove the sterile fronds, or touch the fertile ones: the surface hairs are very easily removed and do not grow again.

Propagation Young plants naturally grow from the stolons or runners which the parent plant sends out. Detach these and pot up in a basket filled with 2 parts peat, 1 part loam and 1 part sphagnum moss. If growing the plant on bark, pack the roots with sphagnum moss and fix to the support with wires; these may be removed once the sterile fronds have attached themselves firmly. Basket-grown plants should be given an annual spring top-dressing of 2 parts peat, 1 part loam and a little bone meal.

Problems Any problems that arise are likely to be the result of incorrect care – insufficient humidity in hot dry conditions or overwatering in winter. Avoid damaging the fronds by overhandling.

See also *Ferns*, page 14-15.

PLATYCERIUM BIFURCATUM

PLUMBAGO CAPENSIS

South Africa
90-120cm (3-4ft)

A charming, short climber with delicate pale blue flowers borne in terminal clusters, 22-30cm (9-12in) in length, on long, slender, lax stems from April to September. With regular pruning *P. capensis* can also be grown as a bushy specimen plant, but will otherwise need training on to supports.

Conditions Grow in good light but shaded from direct sun. Temperatures should be cool to moderate in summer, with a winter minimum of 7°C (45°F). Give higher temperatures of 13-16°C (55-60°F) until December to encourage a longer flowering display the following season. Provide as much fresh air as possible during the summer. Plants will benefit from a period outdoors during warm weather. Support plants with canes or wires.

Care Water liberally from April until after flowering. Keep just moist through winter until the new shoots start to appear, then gradually increase watering. Give a liquid feed at fortnightly intervals from May to September.

Pruning After flowering cut back all shoots by two-thirds.

Potting on In spring when necessary, normally every year; use John Innes No. 3 potting compost.

Propagation In July take heeled cuttings of non-flowering shoots, 7-10cm (3-4in) long. Pot in equal quantities of sand and peat and keep in temperatures of 16-18°C (60-65°F) until rooted.

Problems Leaf fall in winter is the result of low temperatures. Very slow growth and yellowing of leaves may indicate root knot eelworms, which form swollen galls. If treated promptly this will not necessarily affect the whole plant.

POLYANTHUS

British Isles
15-20cm (6-8in)

Well-known winter and spring-flowering plants which come in a variety of colours. The Pacific strain makes particularly good indoor pot plants with large flowers in brilliant shades of blue, yellow, red, pink and white. The flowers grow in trusses on long stems above the rosette of soft, light green leaves. Plants flower naturally from early spring, but are frequently forced into flower before Christmas.

Conditions Grow in a well-lit area shaded from direct sun. Give cool temperatures of not more that 16°C (60°F) during the growing season. In warm conditions, place the pot on wet pebbles or sink it in a container of moist peat.

Care Keep the compost moist at all times during the flowering season. Give a liquid feed once a week as the plants are coming into flower, but not during flowering. Deadhead regularly, and place the plant outside after flowering.

Potting on Polyanthus are normally grown for a single season as indoor plants, but can be planted in the garden after flowering, and they will continue to flower and increase each year.

Propagation From seed sown in February and March.

Problems Normally the result of incorrect treatment. Yellowing foliage means conditions are too hot and dry. Short flowering period is usually due to too much heat, but failure to remove dead flowers will prevent new flower heads being produced. Leaves

PLUMBAGO CAPENSIS

with black edges or brown spots are normally a sign of low temperatures. Keep plants away from cold windowsills, where they may get frosted.

PTERIS CRETICA

**South-west Europe, India, Japan
Ribbon fern
30-45cm (1-1½ft)**

A delightful fern with long, ribbon-like pinnae (leaflets) which are often divided at their ends, and sometimes crested or frilled. 'Albolineata' is a variegated form which has a white central band on each pinna. This plant makes a good subject for a bottle garden.

Conditions Grow in a draught-free position with good indirect light. Maintain a constant temperature of between 13 and 21°C (55-70°F), with a winter minimum of 7°C (45°F). Provide a constantly humid atmosphere by placing pots on damp gravel or sinking them in moist peat. Mist around plants daily in hot dry weather. Keep away from sources of direct heat and avoid fumes.

Care Keep compost evenly moist throughout the year, reducing the frequency of watering in winter. Give fortnightly liquid feeds during the growing season. Remove any dead or damaged fronds.

Potting on In spring, pot on into John Innes No. 2 potting compost with added peat, or into equal parts moss peat, peat-based compost and sharp sand.

Propagation By division of rhizomes, making sure each section has some roots and fronds; or from spores sown in March – these produce fast-growing plants.

Problems Usually the result of incorrect treatment. Keep plants in humid conditions and do not overwater. Fading of leaf variegation may occur if plants are exposed to sun or light that is too bright.

See also *Ferns*, page 13-14.

POLYANTHUS

PTERIS CRETICA

REBUTIA MINUSCULA

REBUTIA MINUSCULA

South America
2·5cm (1in)

Rebutias are a group of miniature globular cacti, some with spines or bristles, none more than 12cm (5in) high. They flower easily and profusely from an early age and in a wide range of colours; the flowers are trumpet-shaped, large in proportion to the plant, and unusual in that they grow from the base of the stem. Each flower lasts a week, and a succession of them nearly covers the plants all summer long. The diminutive *R. minuscula*, which is the earliest to flower, has red flowers as large as the plant itself, and white bristles.

Conditions Give a position in good light and full sun. Temperatures should be warm in summer and cool in winter – around 4·5-7°C (40-45°F).

Care Water sparingly in summer, allowing the soil to become touch-dry in between waterings. Withhold water in winter. These plants need little encouragement to flower, and one liquid feed of a high-potassium fertilizer in the spring should be enough.

Potting on In spring if the pot is filled with roots, repot into shallow pots or dishes, using John Innes No. 2 potting compost with added sand for drainage.

Propagation Because of their vigorous flowering habit, rebutias tend to be short-lived, exhausting themselves within a few years. To keep a good supply of flowering plants it is advisable to propagate annually from the many offsets produced, or from seed. Plants will often flower the first or second year after sowing.

Problems Generally trouble-free if the plant is not overwatered and is kept cool and dry in winter.

See also *Cacti and Succulents*, page 21-22.

RHIPSALIDOPSIS GAERTNERI

Brazil
Easter cactus
30-45cm (1-1½ft)

Sometimes known as *Schlumbergera gaertneri*, this well-known 'leaf cactus' is an epiphyte which grows on forest trees in its natural habitat. The succulent, flattened, leaf-like stems are composed of dull green pads with notched edges. Trumpet-shaped bright red flowers appear profusely in spring. Arched stems make the plants ideal for hanging baskets.

Conditions Grow in a well-lit position out of direct sun. The plant needs warm to average temperatures when actively growing and flowering, and lower temperatures of around 13-16°C (55-60°F) when resting.

Care Keep compost just moist from the end of September to the beginning of February when the plant will be resting. Increase watering slightly from February to the end of March, or until the flower buds have begun to form. At this stage water plants liberally whenever the compost begins to dry out. After flowering, harden off plants by placing them outside in a shady position, where they will grow new pads. Use rainwater whenever possible in hard water areas, and mist stems frequently while inside. Never move plants once buds have started to form, and give weak liquid feeds once a week until they come into flower.

Potting on In mid-September when plants are brought inside; use equal parts leaf mould and fine gravel.

RHIPSALIDOPSIS GAERTNERI

Propagation By stem cuttings of terminal pads in summer. Allow cut surfaces to heal for a few days before potting up in a mixture of sand and peat.

Problems Generally trouble-free

RHOEO DISCOLOR

Central America
Boat lily
30cm (1ft)

An unusual and attractive foliage plant with stiff, sword-shaped leaves which are glossy dark green above and purple below. In young plants the leaves form a rosette which later develops a short stem as the plant matures. The lateral shoots which grow from the stem should be removed if the plant is being grown as a specimen, but will look good in a hanging basket. Small white flowers in purple boat-shaped bracts grow from the bases of the lower leaves.

Conditions Grow in light shade in summer and good light in winter, and away from draughts. Provide average warmth and some humidity in summer, with a minimum winter temperature of 7-10°C (45-50°F).

Care Water liberally in summer and keep the compost just moist in winter. A degree of humidity is needed in the summer and the surrounding air should be misted regularly. Give a fortnightly liquid feed from May to September, and remove dead flowers and leaves promptly.

Potting on In April, annually or when necessary; use John Innes No. 2 or a peat-based compost.

Propagation Plants have a tendency to deteriorate after a few years, but are not too difficult to propagate from 7·5cm (3in) cuttings of basal shoots taken in spring. Pot up individually and place on a warm, shaded windowsill at a minimum temperature of 16°C (60°F).

Problems Generally trouble-free.

RHOEO DISCOLOR

RHOICISSUS RHOMBOIDEA

Natal
Grape ivy
1·2-1·8m (4-6ft)

An attractive and vigorous climbing plant ideal for difficult shaded corners. The dense, dark green, shiny leaves are composed of three irregularly shaped, toothed leaflets. The stems, which bear tendrils, become woody with age but are covered with tiny brown hairs when young. This is a very amenable plant which does well in a variety of situations. If grown as a climber it will need some support; however, placed high up on a shelf it will trail down and is an ideal plant for introducing a further tier of interest to a room.

Conditions Grow in a cool, semi-shaded position in summer, with slightly more light in winter. The plant tolerates a wide range of temperatures, with a winter minimum of 7°C (45°F). Provide support for tendrils to cling to.

Care Water freely in summer, sparingly in winter; avoid waterlogging or standing in water. Feed fortnightly during the growing season and mist the leaves occasionally to increase humidity, particularly in a hot dry atmosphere. Pinch out tips to encourage growth from the base.

Potting on Normally necessary annually, until the plant is in a 23cm (9in) pot, then top-dress every April. Use John Innes No. 2 or a soil-less compost.

Propagation Take stem cuttings with two leaves attached, and put several cuttings in each pot to produce full, bushy plants.

Problems Brown patches on leaves are probably a result of exposure to direct sun. Shrivelled, yellowing and falling leaves indicate overwatering and may lead to rotting if not corrected. Brown, dry leaves indicate insufficient moisture in the air; keep the leaves misted. Mildew on the leaves is a sign of waterlogging or inadequate drainage.

RHOICISSUS RHOMBOIDEA

SAINTPAULIA IONANTHA

South Africa
African violet
7·5-10cm (3-4in)

Perfectly simple, four-petalled, purple-blue flowers with yellow centres grow on a rosette of rounded velvety leaves. Many hybrids have been developed, with single and double blooms and shades ranging from white to pink and mauve. Flowers are freely borne over a long period.

Conditions Grow in a position of bright light throughout the year, but keep away from direct sun. Temperatures should be warm in summer and not less than 16°C (60°F) in winter. Provide a very humid atmosphere. Surround the pot with moist peat or place on wet pebbles, and mist the surrounding air frequently. Do not spray the leaves or flowers directly – they mark very easily. Use rainwater wherever possible in hard water areas; saintpaulias dislike alkaline conditions. Give winter-flowering plants additional (artificial) light during the evenings, but do not put strong lights too near, as the foliage is easily scorched.

Care Keep the compost moist at all times but never allow it to become soggy. To avoid wetting the leaves, either water below the foliage or from underneath, using soft tepid water. Give mature plants fortnightly liquid feeds from May to September, using a low-nitrogen fertilizer which will not encourage leaf growth at the expense of flowers. Remove dead flowers with stalks and foliage immediately. Suckers will form round the base of mature plants, and these should be pinched off.

Potting on Only when absolutely necessary; Saintpaulias flower more freely when their pots are full of roots. Grow in a compost which is equal parts lime-free loam, peat, sand and leaf mould, or in a soil-less compost. Avoid compressing compost when repotting – the plants need a freely draining, well-aerated medium.

Propagation From leaf cuttings with 5cm (2in) of stalk attached. Place in 7·5cm (3in) plastic pots in equal quantities of peat and sand, or simply place in water where the roots will quickly develop. May also be grown from seed.

Problems Usually due to incorrect treatment. Yellowing leaves may indicate incorrect watering, overfeeding or lack of humidity. Pale green leaves with long stalks and curled leaf edges are caused by low temperatures. Brown patches on leaves are caused by watering with cold water. Crisp straw-coloured patches are caused by direct sunlight. Mouldy leaves and flowers are a symptom of botrytis disease. There are several possible causes of lack of flowers, the most probable being insufficient light, but also possible are dry air, cold air, too frequent repotting, failure to remove side shoots, moving the plant, or too much nitrogen in the fertilizer.

SANSEVIERIA TRIFASCIATA 'LAURENTII'

West Africa
Mother-in-law's tongue
45cm (1½ft)

This is a tough succulent which will survive in almost any conditions. Erect, fleshy, sword-shaped stems grow in clumps directly from the compost; they are dark green, mottled with grey-green transverse bands, and have creamy-yellow margins.

Conditions Prefers bright light with some shade from strong sun, and needs average temperatures, winter minimum 10°C (50°F).

Care Water moderately from spring until autumn and allow the compost to dry out between waterings. In winter, water infrequently (every one to two months), and avoid

SANSEVIERIA TRIFASCIATA

wetting the centre of the plant. The thick stems make the plant drought-tolerant, but the roots will rot easily if overwatered in winter. Give fortnightly liquid feeds from May to September.

Potting on Sansevierias are slow-growing plants – only a few fresh leaves will appear each year, and potting on is seldom necessary. When the pot is packed with roots and leaves, pot on in a peat-based compost.

Propagation Divide the plant when potting on, or sever suckers from the parent plant when two or three leaves have formed.

Problems Rotting at the base, with leaves yellowing and dying back, is normally due to overwatering in winter. If part of the plant is still healthy, cut this away, repot and keep it warm and dry. Curling leaves forming a tubular shape are the result of underwatering in summer.

SAINTPAULIA IONANTHA

SAXIFRAGA SARMENTOSA 'TRICOLOR'

China
Mother of thousands
22-30cm (9-12in)

Tiny plantlets are freely produced on thread-like red runners, which cascade from the parent plant. Small, white, starry flowers appear in summer. *Saxifraga sarmentosa* 'Tricolor' has leaves which are charmingly edged pinky-white, and it is a little less vigorous than the type. Grow the plants in small hanging pots, or trailing over the edge of containers, and in a spot where the delicate foliage will not be overlooked. This is another plant that does well when placed high up on a shelf, from which the runners can cascade down to a depth of about 60cm (2ft) in favourable conditions.

Conditions Give a light or semi-shaded position and warm to moderate temperatures, with a winter minimum of 7°C (45°F). It likes a slightly humid atmosphere, particularly in the summer months, and will benefit from regular spraying with tepid water.

Care Water freely from April to September, and more sparingly in winter, and give fortnightly liquid feeds.

Potting on Every other year in April. Use John Innes No. 2 potting compost, which must not be compacted or drainage will be impaired.

Propagation From plantlets in April and May. Keep them attached to the parent plant until rooted, and water sparingly during this period.

Problems Mainly due to incorrect treatment. Yellowing leaves are caused by overwatering and poor drainage, and there is little chance of recovery once the roots have begun to rot. Runners becoming brown is an indication that either the plant is being kept too dry, or that the atmosphere lacks humidity.

SCHEFFLERA ACTINOPHYLLA

Australasia
Umbrella tree
To 2m (6ft)

A handsome foliage plant with long, glossy, oval leaflets growing in radiating groups from long leaf stalks. The leaflets increase in number as the plant matures. Position the plant where it will have room to expand in both height and spread: although it does not usually do so when grown as a pot plant, this species is capable of reaching a height of 3m (10ft).

Conditions Place in a bright position away from direct sun in summer, but in maximum light during the winter. Give average warmth, not less than 13°C (55°F), and avoid draughts. Maintain a humid atmosphere by misting the leaves frequently.

Care Keep the compost moist in spring and summer, but reduce watering in win-

SAXIFRAGA SARMENTOSA 'TRICOLOR'

SCHEFFLERA ACTINOPHYLLA

Conditions Keep in a bright spot, such as a well-lit windowsill, but avoid direct sun. Give warmth, with temperatures of 16-21°C (60-70°F) from September to April while buds are forming and the plant is in flower.

Care Water freely when plants are in bud and in flower, and mist regularly around them. After flowering, between April and May, continue to water well but allow the compost to dry out slightly in between waterings. During the summer place in a cool shaded spot inside, or – better still – outside, so plants can harden off. Bring into warmer temperatures in September, and water cautiously until buds appear. Do not move plants once buds have formed. Give a weekly liquid feed from bud formation until flowering begins. To bring plants into flower earlier, from September on keep plants inside, in a spot where they are exposed only to natural daylight, and are in darkness in the evening.

Potting on After the resting period, in spring, repot in equal parts loam, peat and leaf mould with a little bone meal added.

Propagation From stem cuttings of terminal pads, taken along the joint. Allow cut surfaces to heal for two days before potting up in a peat and sand mixture. Pot into normal compost when rooted.

Problems Generally trouble-free, provided correct treatment is given.

ter. Give a liquid feed every month from April to September.

Potting on *S. actinophylla* is a slow-growing plant but larger containers will encourage growth. Pot on regularly until a 15cm (8in) pot size is reached, then top-dress every other year. Use John Innes No. 2 compost.

Propagation Stem cuttings may be taken or seeds sown; however, home cultivation is very difficult.

Problems Scale insects may attack. Loss of lower leaves is normal on maturing plants. Avoid overwatering.

SCHLUMBERGERA × 'BUCKLEYI'

Brazil
Christmas cactus
15-22cm (6-9in)

The most common hybrid of the schlumbergera group of Christmas-flowering forest cacti, with large, cerise, trumpet-shaped flowers which appear at any time from November to January. Other hybrids flower in shades of pink, red, mauve and orange. Freely branching, leaf-like stems are jointed into pads, which have round indentations along the margins. Plants are usually bought in bud, about to flower.

SCHLUMBERGERA × 'BUCKLEYI'

Scindapsus aureus

Solomon Islands
Devil's ivy
2m (6ft)

Also known as *Rhaphidophora aurea*, this is a variegated climber on firm stems which has two leaf forms. Mature leaves are up to 30cm (1ft) long, bright green strongly marked with yellow, and heart-shaped. The juvenile leaves are broad, spear-shaped and less than a third of that size. Varieties are available with different proportions of green and yellow in the leaf variegation. Mature parts of the plant are sometimes rooted and sold as large-leaved plants, but the leaves revert to their juvenile forms as growth continues. Devil's ivy is usually seen as a climber, but can be allowed to trail.

Conditions Provide a bright position away from direct sun during the summer, but allow maximum light in winter to keep leaf variegation in full colour. Temperatures should be warm with a high level of humidity in the air in summer, and a minimum of 13°C (55°F) in winter. The plant puts out aerial roots for moisture and anchorage, so provide it with a constantly moist sphagnum moss stick.

Care Keep compost evenly moist during the summer, slightly drier in winter; mist regularly during warm weather. Give monthly liquid feeds from May to September.

Pruning Remove growing tips to encourage side growth, and cut back oversized plants in June.

Potting on Every two or three years in April if large plants are wanted; otherwise top-dress plants over 1·2m (4ft) high every two years. Use John Innes No. 2 or a peat-based compost.

Propagation Take 10cm (4in) cuttings of tip growths or basal shoots from May to July. Place in equal quantities of peat and sand and provide some bottom heat. When rooted pot into 3in pots.

Problems Curled limp leaves and limp stems indicate temperatures which are too low. Brown leaf edges and surface spots indicate underwatering; do not let the root ball dry out. Brown shrivelled tops indicate dry air; plunge pots in moistened peat, and mist regularly. Yellowing and falling leaves together with rotting stems are normally the result of overwatering.

Senecio cruentus

Canary Islands
Cineraria
45cm (1½ft)

Popularly known as cinerarias, these winter and spring-flowering members of the senecio group make colourful temporary houseplants and are available in a wide variety of sizes, colours and forms. The compact multiflora 'Nana' has large, broad-petalled flowers; 'Stellata' is wider-growing with many small, narrow-petalled flowers. Colours include white, lavender, blue, mauve, red, pink and many bicolours; the smaller forms tend to flower earlier, and the plants can be grown in succession to provide colour from Christmas to June.

Conditions Grow in a semi-shaded position in summer, well-lit in winter. Cool humid conditions are preferred, with a minimum winter temperature of 7°C (45°F). Plunge the pots in peat or place on damp pebbles. A well-drained soil is essential – the most frequent cause of plant collapse is waterlogging.

Care Water frequently but carefully, allowing the compost to dry slightly in between waterings. Give fortnightly liquid feeds between the time the buds appear and flowering begins. Remove dead flowers and leaves promptly by twisting off. Plants should be discarded after flowering.

SCINDAPSUS AUREUS

SENECIO CRUENTUS

Propagation From seed, but this is not easy, and is not really worth attempting except in a greenhouse.

Potting on Plants can generally be left in the containers they were bought in, but by the time they are ready to flower they will have become very pot-bound and will require more watering.

Problems Normally due to incorrect treatment. Yellowing foliage with healthy crowns indicates high temperatures – which should never rise above 16°C (60°F). A short flowering period is due to too much heat, incorrect watering or to dry air. Rotting at the base (black neck disease) results from overwatering. Grey mould on leaves is botrytis disease; remove dead flowers and leaves promptly.

SENECIO MACROGLOSSUS 'VARIEGATUS'

**South Africa
Cape ivy
1m (3ft) or more**

A vigorous climber or trailer with waxy, ivy-shaped leaves, green variegated with gold. Daisy-like flowers may appear during the winter. Plants tend to become ragged and lose their shape if allowed to grow over 1·2m (4ft).

Conditions Grows best in a brightly lit spot shaded from direct sun, but will tolerate some shade. Give an average temperature, with a winter minimum of 10°C (50°F), and some humidity. Provide support if grown as a climber.

Care Keep compost moist in summer, but avoid waterlogging. Always use tepid water, rainwater if possible in hard water areas. Water sparingly in winter. Mist the leaves frequently to maintain slightly humid conditions, and give a liquid feed once a fortnight from April to September. Pinch out growing tips to encourage a bushy shape.

Potting on Every two years, to a final pot size of 30cm (10in), using John Innes No. 2 potting compost.

Propagation Take stem cuttings in spring and summer to replace straggly plants.

Problems Aphids may attack the tender tip growth.

SENECIO MACROGLOSSUS 'VARIEGATUS'

SINNINGIA SPECIOSA 'FYFIANA'

Brazil
Gloxinia
30cm (1ft)

The florists' gloxinia, with its large, velvety, dark green leaves and huge trumpet-shaped blooms, makes a flamboyant houseplant. Leaves are arranged in rosettes around a central cluster of frilly-edged flowers in shades of red, purple, pink and white. The deeper shades often have white margins. A plant with plenty of buds will continue to bloom for up to two months.

Conditions Grow in a bright, draught-free place away from direct sun. Give a warm humid atmosphere with a minimum winter temperature of 16°C (60°F). Stand the pot on a tray of wet pebbles or sink in moistened peat.

Care during flowering Allow the surface of the compost to dry out before giving the plant a really good soak in tepid water. Since flowers and leaves are easily marked, it is better to water the plant from beneath, or by immersion. Mist the surrounding air frequently. Feed fortnightly when the buds appear and until the end of the flowering period. Remove dead flowers regularly to prevent them rotting the brittle, easily damaged leaves.

Care after flowering Watering should be stopped when the leaves have turned yellow. When they have died back remove the tuber and store in a mixture of dry peat and sand in a temperature of around 10°C (50°F). Pot up in spring, ensuring that the concave surface of the tuber is uppermost. Use a 12·5cm (5in) pot filled with a moist peat-based compost. Keep in a temperature of 21°C (70°F) and water sparingly until the plant comes into growth. Tubers can be kept for three years before being discarded.

Propagation Sow seeds in January, or pot up young shoots with a piece of the tuber attached.

SINNINGIA SPECIOSA 'FYFIANA'

Problems Plant collapse, accompanied by softening and rotting of the tuber, is caused by overwatering or bad drainage; when planting tubers ensure that the top is level with the surface of the compost, otherwise water will collect in the hollow. Buds failing to open is normally the result of insufficient humidity or cold draughts. Pale elongated leaves are due either to inadequate light or to watering with cold water.

SOLANUM CAPSICASTRUM

Brazil
Winter cherry
30-45cm (1-1½ft)

A compact bushy plant, well known for its bright cherry-sized red berries at Christmas time. Tiny, white, star-shaped flowers appear in June and July. The fruits, dark green at first, ripen through yellow to red, and given the right conditions will last until February. It is normally bought as an annual but can be grown on for a number of years. Keep the berries away from children – they are poisonous.

Conditions Grow in a well-lit position with some sun. The plant needs a cool temperature, around 10-13°C (50-55°F), in winter to prevent early berry drop. Provide some humidity.

Care Keep compost moist at all times. Place plants outside from June to September and mist regularly, especially when flowering, to encourage setting of fruits.

two flowering periods – early spring and early summer. Its colouring makes *S. africana* a perfect foil for group planting.

Conditions Grow in a well-lit and well-ventilated position away from direct sun during the summer, and allow maximum light during the winter to ensure spring flowering. Cool summer temperatures will induce summer flowering, and give a minimum of 7°C (45°F) during the winter. Maintain a slightly humid atmosphere.

Care Keep compost moist at all times: plants may need watering daily in summer, but avoid overwatering in winter. Mist around the leaves frequently in warm conditions. Give a weekly liquid feed from March to September, and clean the leaves by standing plants outside in warm rain.

Pruning The plant is a vigorous grower: check growth and encourage side shoots by pinching out the tips of young plants. Cut back stems after flowering.

Potting on This may be necessary twice a year for vigorous young plants, or annually in spring; use John Innes No. 3 potting compost.

Propagation 7·5-10cm (3-4in) cuttings of young plants, taken when they are cut back after spring flowering, are easily rooted. Plants which become too tall or leggy should be discarded and new plants grown on.

Problems Generally trouble-free.

SOLANUM CAPSICASTRUM

Give regular liquid feeds from April until the fruit begins to ripen.

Pruning In March cut growth back by one-third.

Potting on Normally necessary annually; use John Innes No. 2 potting compost.

Propagation Sow seed in February.

Problems Early leaf fall indicates overwatering. Early berry drop indicates either too little light, or hot dry air.

SPARMANNIA AFRICANA

South Africa
House lime
1m (3ft)

The pale green, slightly downy, heart-shaped leaves grow to 15cm (6in) across. Large, white-petalled flowers with protruding yellow stamens grow in umbels and normally appear in the second year when the plant has reached 60cm (2ft). There are

SPARMANNIA AFRICANA

SPATHIPHYLLUM WALLISII

SPATHIPHYLLUM WALLISII

Colombia
Peace lily
22-30cm (9-12in)

A striking plant belonging to the arum lily family, with glossy, dark green, lanceolate leaves on long slender stems, which grow in clumps directly from the compost. The flower heads are creamy central spikes surrounded by white oval spathes, and are held high above the foliage on tall, erect stems. Its exotic appearance and exception-ally long season of interest make this one of the most rewarding specimen plants, as it is not too difficult to grow as long as it can be kept out of draughts, direct summer sun and winter cold. The flowering period is from May to August. The taller hybrid 'Mauna Loa' flowers more freely for a longer period, but is a less hardy and therefore more demanding plant.

Conditions Give a draught-free position in semi-shade during the summer, direct sun in winter. Constant warmth and a humid atmosphere are needed, though *S. wallisii* will tolerate a winter temperature of 10°C (50°F). Plunge pots in damp peat or place on wet pebbles.

Care Water freely during the summer, twice a day in very hot weather, and less freely in winter, but always keep the compost moist. Mist frequently throughout the year, and give a liquid feed every ten days from late March to September. Clean leaves occasionally with moist cotton wool to keep them free of dust.

Potting on Normally necessary every year in April until a 12·5cm (5in) pot size has been reached, after which the plants should be top-dressed annually. Use a peat-based compost.

Propagation By division of the clumps in spring at potting time.

Problems Strong summer sun will damage leaves. Plants will deteriorate rapidly if the minimum temperature is not maintained. Given the correct treatment this plant is normally free from pests and diseases, although insect pests such as red spider mite can damage plants weakened by lack of attention.

STREPTOCARPUS × HYBRIDUS

South Africa
Cape primrose
20-30cm (9-12in)

Attractive and easy flowering plants related to gloxinia and flowering throughout spring and summer. The flowers are foxglove-like, coloured white, pink, blue, purple or red, and are carried on tall stems above large, wrinkled, hairy leaves. Some plants will flower well into the autumn; the particularly popular variety 'Constant nymph' is long-flowering and has blue flowers borne continuously until November in ordinary house conditions.

Conditions Grow in a well-lit and draught-free position out of direct sunlight. Allow some ventilation in warm weather. Tem-

STREPTOCARPUS

peratures should be moderate throughout the flowering period, with an ideal winter temperature of 10°C (50°F).

Care Water freely during the spring and summer, using the immersion method, and allowing the soil surface to dry out slightly in between waterings. Decrease watering in winter to keep compost just moist. Streptocarpus enjoys humidity in the air, but care should be taken to avoid overwetting the leaves when misting, as they are easily damaged. It will help to maintain an adequate level of atmospheric humidity if the plants are stood on a water-filled gravel tray. Give a weak liquid feed at 10 day intervals between May and September.

Potting on Annually in spring, into a peat-based compost or John Innes No. 2.

Propagation From seed sown in January to flower in autumn, or in March to flower the following year in summer. Alternatively, take leaf cuttings in summer.

Problems Yellowing and rotting leaves are a result of direct contact with water: avoid pouring water on to leaves when watering or misting. Poor flowering display is probably due to insufficient light.

SYNGONIUM PODOPHYLLUM

Mexico and Panama
Goose foot plant
To 1·2m (4ft) or more

An attractive climber, closely related to the philodendrons and, like them, it dramatically changes form and leaf shape as it matures. Young, strongly variegated, arrow-shaped leaves grow on erect stalks from the compost. With age the stems acquire a climbing habit and develop aerial shoots; the arrow-shaped leaves become lobed and then divided into three, five or eight leaflets and may be up to 30cm (1ft) long. Variegation fades as the plant matures; to retain the juvenile form, remove the climbing stems as they appear. A mature plant will need the support of a sphagnum moss stick. Many variegated varieties exist; *S. p.* 'Green God' is probably the most attractive.

Conditions Place in a well-lit area, but avoid direct sun. Give year-round warm to moderate temperatures, with a winter minimum of 16°C (60°F). Maintain a constantly humid atmosphere by placing the pot on wet pebbles or sinking it in moist peat.

Care Water thoroughly from April to October, but allow the compost to dry out slightly between waterings. Water sparingly in winter and never allow waterlogging, as the roots rot easily. Mist frequently, and give a liquid feed every fortnight in summer.

Potting on Normally necessary every two years in April. Use a peat-based compost.

Propagation From stem cuttings with aerial shoots attached.

Problems Sudden wilting and shrivelling may occur if the air is too dry or cool.

SYNGONIUM PODOPHYLLUM

TETRASTIGMA VOINIERIANUM

TETRASTIGMA VOINIERIANUM

China
Chestnut vine
To 2·4m (8ft) or more

This is a rampant, large-leaved climber with dusty, chestnut-like leaves and strong tendrils which will attach themselves to any available support; an ideal plant for covering room dividers or screens. Its rate of growth depends on conditions, but it can put on several feet a year. The mature plant produces greenish-yellow flowers.

Conditions Grow in good light but avoid direct summer sun. Give a moderate temperature with a winter minimum of 10°C (50°F). Plants like a slightly humid atmosphere and this can be maintained by frequent misting. Must be supported by a strong framework, otherwise it may fall, taking its support with it.

Care Water freely during the summer and more sparingly in winter. Give liquid feeds every fortnight during the growing period. Pinch out tips occasionally to encourage side shoots.

Potting on Annually in spring until a 30cm (12in) pot size is reached; thereafter the compost should be top-dressed every April. Use John Innes No. 3 compost and place some crocks at the base of the pot to ensure good drainage.

Propagation From stem cuttings with two leaves attached.

Problems Brown patches on leaves are probably due to exposure to direct sun. Shrivelled, yellow, falling leaves are a sign of overwatering, which may in turn lead to rotting if not corrected. Mildew on leaves is a sign of waterlogging or inadequate drainage. Dry brown leaves indicate a lack of humidity.

TOLMIEA MENZIESII

Western USA
Piggy-back plant
To 15cm (6in)

The common name is derived from the way the hairy, maple-like leaves produce young plantlets at the base, and appear to be carrying them. The foliage forms a compact spreading mound with greenish-white, pink-flushed flower spikes growing high above the foliage in June. Being a hardy plant, Tolmiea is quite frequently grown out of doors. As a houseplant it can be overwintered in an unheated room, and will benefit from a spell outside during the warmer months.

Conditions A tolerant plant which prefers a well-lit position, but will grow in shade. Give average temperatures, with a winter minimum of 4·5°C (40°F). Ventilate the room well during summer.

Care Water liberally during the growing season and keep compost just moist in winter. Give a weak liquid feed once a month from April to September, and mist leaves regularly during the summer.

Potting on Normally annually in spring, in John Innes No. 2 or a peat-based compost.

TOLMIEA MENZIESII

TRADESCANTIA BLOSSFELDIANA

Propagation The plantlets naturally weigh down the parent leaf and eventually reach the compost and take root. Pot-grown plants can be easily propagated by removing a parent leaf with a well-developed plantlet attached and rooting it in a separate pot.

Problems Generally trouble-free. Hot dry air may cause infestation by red spider mite.

TRADESCANTIA BLOSSFELDIANA 'VARIEGATA'

Argentina
Wandering Jew
Trailing

This ubiquitous trailing plant has many named varieties with numerous leaf vari-

ations. *T. blossfeldiana* 'Variegata' has a slightly more upright habit than most, with larger leaves and flowers. The dark green, ovate, slightly hairy leaves have a faint purple tinting and strong cream stripes; the undersides of the leaves and the stems are purple. Rose-purple flowers with white 'eyes' appear in May and June. Closely related is *Zebrina pendula*, the silver inch plant, with wide, colourful, silver-striped leaves that are bright red underneath. It is more shade-tolerant than the tradescantias; the stems have an attractive habit of trailing downwards to cover the pot and then 'flicking' upwards again.

Conditions Tradescantias will put up with most conditions, but the resultant weak, straggly growths are too often seen. Grown

in bright light with a minimum winter temperature of 7°C (45°F), the plants will develop good colour variegations and fine forms.

Care Water freely during the growing period but allow the compost to dry out slightly in between waterings. Water sparingly in winter. Pinch out growing tips frequently to encourage bushy growth, and remove the green shoots on variegated plants as soon as they appear. Mist the leaves occasionally and give fortnightly liquid feeds from April to September. Straggly plants are better discarded.

Potting on Normally necessary annually in April. Use John Innes No. 2 or a peat-based compost.

Propagation Stem cuttings will root easily, either in water or directly in the compost, and are best taken in summer. Always place several cuttings in one pot for good full plants.

Problems Generally trouble-free if given correct care and pinched out regularly. In poor light plants may lose their variegation and revert to uniform green.

VRIESIA SPLENDENS

VRIESIA SPLENDENS

South America
Flaming sword
45cm (1½ft)

A group of terrestrial and epiphytic bromeliads with the typical rosette form and water vase. The leaves are thick, strap-shaped and glossy, often strikingly patterned or coloured. *V. splendens* has slender dark green leaves cross-banded with purple, and a sword-shaped flowering stem rising from the centre to a height of about 60cm (2ft), with a sheath of overlapping red bracts and yellow flowers. These generally appear in July and August. These plants need warmth and a high degree of humidity to be successfully grown and flowered in the home. Vriesias are suitable subjects for growing on a bromeliad tree: the roots are wrapped in a ball of sphagnum moss and wired on to a dead branch or piece of driftwood. They must not be allowed to dry out, and will need foliar feeding.

Conditions Grow in a permanent position of light shade. Give warmth all year round, with a minimum temperature of 18°C (65°F), and give high humidity in the surrounding air. Mist frequently with tepid softened water.

Care Keep the central vase always topped up with water, preferably rainwater, and the compost moist. In winter keep the compost on the dry side, but maintain a humid atmosphere. Set pots in containers of moist peat for additional humidity. The plants can be given occasional feeds in the spring and summer, either in the form of a foliar spray, or as a weak liquid solution added to the water in the vase. Do not fertilize when the plant is in full flower.

Potting on Repot into the next pot size every second or third year, or when the roots have filled the pot. Use a mixture of equal parts peat, sphagnum moss or leaf mould, and sand.

Propagation From offsets produced at the base of the plant and detached, with some roots, when they are one-third to half the size of the parent. Allow them to dry for a few days before potting them up individually in the growing compost.

Problems Brown patches on the leaves may be caused by exposure to direct sun. Brown tips on the leaves usually indicate insufficient humidity in the air. Rotting at the base may be due to overwatering of the compost or, if the plant has flowered, to the natural death of the parent rosette. In this case, propagate as above.

See also *Bromeliads*, pages 15-18.

YUCCA ALOIFOLIA

United States
Spanish bayonet
1·2-1·8m (4-6ft)

A familiar specimen plant which is found in two forms as a houseplant. One is the young upright form of *Y. elephantipes*, which has sword-shaped, spiky leaves growing from a central stem, rather like a spiky dracaena; the other is the peculiar but more popular *Y. aloifolia*, with young plants sprouting from sawn-up sections of mature stem.

Conditions Give as much light as possible throughout the year; a south-facing window is ideal. It grows best in cool conditions, with a minimum winter temperature of 7°C (45°F), and benefits from a period outside during the summer in a warm sheltered spot. If this is not possible, allow some ventilation.

Care Water compost well during the summer, allowing it to dry slightly in between waterings. Water sparingly in winter and keep compost just moist. Give a liquid feed every fortnight from April to September, and mist the leaves from time to time.

Potting on Every other year in spring. Use a clay pot to aid stability, and pot in John Innes No. 2 – this is heavier than the soilless composts and will help to balance the plants, which may otherwise become rather top-heavy. For the same reason a clay pot is more suitable than a plastic one.

Propagation From lengths of mature stem. Sections about 5cm (2½in) in diameter, placed in pots of moist compost, will grow roots and shoots. Always plant the end that was originally nearer to the roots in the compost. Propagation of *Y. elephantipes* is by offsets that grow at the base of the plant.

Problems Usually a result of incorrect treatment. Brown tips on the leaves indicate lack of water. Mealy bug and scale insects may attack.

YUCCA ALOIFOLIA

Summary of Houseplant Features

Name	Height	Difficulty	Seasons	Temperature	Light	Humidity	Feature
Abutilon	1·2m (4ft)	★★	1-3	Moderate	L minus S	●●	Specimen
Achimenes	30cm (1ft)	★★	2-3	Warm	L	●●●	Flower
Adiantum	23cm (9in)	★★		Warm	S	●●●●	Terrarium
Aechmea	60cm (2ft)	★★	2-3	Warm	L minus S	●●●	Flower
Agave	15cm (6in)	★		Moderate	L		Succulent
Aglaonema	60cm (2ft)	★		Moderate	S/L	●●●	Foliage
Aloe	30cm (12in)	★★		Warm	L		Succulent
Aphelandra	45cm (1½ft)	★★	2-3	Warm	L minus S	●●●	Foliage & bracts
Araucaria	1·5 (5ft)	★★		Moderate	S/L	●	Specimen
Asparagus	1m (3ft)	★		Moderate	S/L	●●	Foliage
Aspidistra	50cm (20in)	★		Cool	S	●	Specimen
Asplenium	60cm (2ft)	★★		Warm	S	●●●	Specimen
Azalea	60cm (2ft)	★★	4-1	Cool	L minus S	●	Flower
Begonia × 'Lucerna'	1·8m (6ft)	★★	1-2	Moderate	L minus S	●●	Specimen
Begonia rex	30cm (1ft)	★★		Moderate	L minus S	●●	Leaf
Begonia semperflorens	22cm (9in)	★	2-3	Moderate	L minus S	●	Flower
Begonia tuberhybrida	60cm (2ft)	★★	2-3	Moderate	L minus S	●●	Flower
Beloperone	60cm (2ft)	★	1-3	Moderate	L	●●	Bracts
Billbergia	45cm (1½ft)	★	any	Moderate	L minus S	●	Foliage & flower
Caladium	45cm (1½ft)	★★★		Warm	L	●●●●	Foliage
Calathea	60cm (2ft)	★★★		Warm	L minus S	●●●●	Foliage/bottle
Calceolaria	30cm (1ft)	★	1	Cool	S/L	●	Flower
Capsicum	45cm (1½ft)	★★★	4	Cool	L	●●	Berry
Celosia	60cm (2ft)	★	2-3	Cool	L	●	Flower
Ceropegia	100cm (3ft)	★	3	Moderate	S/L	●	Trailing
Chamaedorea	1·4m (4ft)	★		Moderate	S/L	●●	Specimen
Chlorophytum	30cm (12in)	★		Moderate	S/L	●	Hanging

Key

Difficulty	Season	Temperature	Light	Humidity
★ easy	1 spring	Warm 16-21°C (60-70°F)	L good light	● some humidity
★★ more difficult	2 summer	Moderate 10-16°C (50-60°F)	L minus S good light, shaded from sun	●● more humidity
★★★ difficult	3 autumn	Cool 7-10°C (45-50°F)	S/L semi-light	●●● humid
	4 winter		S shade	●●●● very humid

Name	Height	Difficulty	Seasons	Temperature	Light	Humidity	Feature
Chrysanthemum	30cm (12in)	★	3	Cool	S/L	●	Flower
Cissus	2·4m (8ft)	★		Moderate	S/L	●●	Climber
Clivia	60cm (2ft)	★★		Cool	S/L	●	Flowering bulb
Codiaeum	60cm (2ft)	★★★		Warm	L	●●●●	Foliage
Coffea	1·2m (4ft)	★★		Moderate	S/L	●●	Specimen
Coleus	45cm (1½ft)	★★★		Moderate	L	●●	Foliage
Cordyline	75cm (2½ft)	★★★		Warm	S/L	●●●	Specimen
Crassula	1m (3ft)	★		Cool	L		Succulent
Ctenanthe	30cm (1ft)	★★★		Warm	S/L	●●●●	Leaf & bottle
Cyclamen	45cm (1½ft)	★★★	3-4	Cool	S/L	●●	Flower
Cyperus	75cm (2½ft)	★		Moderate	S/L	●●●	Specimen
Cyrtomium	60cm (2ft)	★		Moderate	S	●	Fern
Davallia	45cm (1½ft)	★		Moderate	L minus S	●●	Fern
Dieffenbachia	1m (3ft)	★★★		Warm	S/L	●●●●	Foliage
Dizygotheca	1·2 (4ft)	★★★		Warm	L	●●●●	Specimen
Dracaena deremensis	1·2m (4ft)	★★		Moderate	S/L	●●	Specimen
Dracaena godseffiana	60cm (2ft)	★★		Moderate	L	●	Foliage
Dracaena marginata	1·5m (5ft)	★★		Moderate	S/L	●●	Specimen
Dracaena sanderiana	45cm (1½ft)	★★		Moderate	S/L	●●	Specimen
Epiphyllum	90cm (3ft)	★★	1-2	Moderate	L minus S	●●	Flowering
Euonymus	2m (6ft)	★		Cool	L minus S	●	Specimen
Euphorbia millii	60cm (2ft)	★★	3-4	Moderate	L		Flowering succulent
Euphorbia pulcherrima	45cm (1½ft)	★★	4	Warm	L	●●	Bracts/flowering
Exacum	30cm (12in)	★	2-3	Moderate	L minus S	●	Flowering
Fatshedera	1·8m (6ft)	★		Cool	S	●	Climbing
Fatsia japonica	1m (3ft)	★		Cool	S/L	●	Specimen
Ficus benjamina	1·8m (6ft)	★★		Moderate	L minus S	●●	Specimen
Ficus elastica	2·4m (8ft)	★★		Moderate	L minus S	●	Specimen
Ficus lyrata	1·2m (4ft)	★★		Warm	S/L	●●	Specimen
Ficus pumila	60cm (2ft)	★★		Moderate	S	●●●	Creeping/trailing

Name	Height	Difficulty	Seasons	Temperature	Light	Humidity	Feature
Fittonia	15cm (6in)	★★★		Warm	S	●●●●	Bottle
Gardenia	1m (3ft)	★★★	2	Warm	L minus S	●●●	Flowering
Grevillea	1m (3ft)	★		Cool	L minus S	●	Specimen
Guzmania	45cm (1½ft)	★★	any	Warm	S/L	●●●	Flowering
Gynura	60cm (2ft)	★		Moderate	L minus S	●	Trailing
Haworthia	15cm (6in)	★		Warm	L minus S		Succulent
Hedera	1m (3ft)	★★		Moderate	S	●●	Trailer/climber
Helxine	prostrate	★		Moderate	L minus S	●	Creeper
Heptapleurum	90cm (34in)	★★		Warm	L minus S	●	Specimen
Hippeastrum	75cm (2½ft)	★	4	Warm	L minus S	●●●	Specimen
Howea	4m (12ft)	★		Warm	S/L	●●	Specimen
Hoya bella	30cm (12in)	★★★	1-2	Warm	S/L minus S	●●●	Flowering
Hoya carnosa	5m (16ft)	★★	1-2	Moderate	L minus S	●●	Flowering climber
Hydrangea	60cm (2ft)	★★	1-2	Cool	S/L minus S		Flowering
Hypoestes	45cm (1½ft)	★★		Warm	L minus S	●●	Foliage
Impatiens	60cm (2ft)	★	1-4	Moderate	L minus S	●	Flowering
Jasminum	3m (10ft)	★	1 & 4	Moderate	L	●	Flowering climber
Kalanchoë	25cm (10in)	★	4	Moderate	L		Flowering succulent
Lilium longiflorum	1m (3ft)	★★	2	Cool	L minus S		Flowering bulb
Mammillaria	15cm (6in)	★	1-2	Warm	L		Flowering cactus
Maranta	20cm (8in)	★★★		Warm	S/L	●●●	Foliage
Monstera	2·4m (8ft)	★		Moderate	S/L	●	Specimen
Nephrolepis	60cm (2ft)	★★		Warm	S/L	●●●	Hanging/specimen
Pelargonium spp.	60cm (2ft)	★	1, 2, 3	Moderate	L		Flowering
Pellaea	spreading	★		Moderate	S/L	●●	Creeper/trailer
Peperomia caperata	25cm (10in)	★★★		Warm	L minus S	●●●●	Bottle
Peperomia magnoliaefolia	20cm (8in)	★★		Warm	S/L	●●	Foliage
Philodendron bipinnatifidum	1m (3ft)	★		Warm	S/L	●	Specimen
Philodendron hastatum	1·5m (5ft)	★★		Moderate	S/L	●●	Specimen
Philodendron scandens	2m (6ft)	★		Moderate	S/L	●	Climber/trailer

Name	Height	Difficulty	Seasons	Temperature	Light	Humidity	Feature
Phoenix	3m (10ft)	★★		Cool	S/L	●	Palm/specimen
Pilea cadierei	30cm (12in)	★★		Warm	L minus S	●●	Foliage
Pilea nummularifolia	prostrate	★★		Warm	L minus S	●●	Creeper
Platycerium	75cm (2½ft)	★★		Warm	L minus S	●●	Hanging/feature
Plumbago	1·2m (4ft)	★★	2-3	Cool	L minus S	●	Flowering
Polyanthus	20cm (8in)	★	4-1	Cool	L minus S		Flowering
Pteris	45cm (1½ft)	★★		Warm	S/L	●●●	Fern/bottle
Rebutia	2·5cm (1in)	★	1-2	Warm	L		Flowering cactus
Rhipsalidopsis	45cm (1½ft)	★★	1	Warm	L minus S	●	Flowering cactus
Rhoeo	30cm (12in)	★★		Moderate	S/L	●●	Foliage
Rhoicissus	1·8m (6ft)	★		Cool	S/L	●	Climber/trailer
Saintpaulia	10cm (4in)	★★		Warm	L minus S	●●	Flowering
Sansevieria	45cm (1½ft)	★★		Moderate	S/L		Succulent/foliage
Saxifraga	30cm (12in)	★		Moderate	S/L	●	Trailing
Schefflera	2m (6ft)	★★		Moderate	L minus S	●	Specimen
Schlumbergera	22cm (9in)	★★	4	Warm	L minus S	●	Flowering cactus
Scindapsus	2m (6ft)	★★		Warm	L minus S	●●	Climber/trailer
Senecio cruentus	45cm (1½ft)	★	1-2	Cool	L minus S		Flowering
Senecio macroglossus	1m (3ft)	★★		Moderate	L minus S	●	Climber
Sinningia	30cm (12in)	★★	2	Warm	L minus S	●●	Flowering
Solanum	45cm (1½ft)	★★	4	Cool	L	●	Berries
Sparmannia	1m (3ft)	★		Cool	L minus S	●	Foliage
Spathiphyllum	30cm (12in)	★★	2	Cool	S/L	●●	Flowering/foliage
Streptocarpus	30cm (12in)	★	1-2	Moderate	L minus S	●●	Flowering
Syngonium	1·2m (4ft)	★★		Moderate	L minus S	●●	Climber/specimen
Tetrastigma	2·4m (8ft)	★		Moderate	L minus S	●	Climber
Tolmiea	15cm (6in)	★		Moderate	S/L	●	Trailer
Tradescantia	30cm (1ft)	★		Moderate	L minus S	●	Trailer
Vriesia	45cm (1½ft)	★★	2	Warm	S/L	●●	Flowering bromeliad
Yucca	1·8m (6ft)	★		Cool	L		Specimen

Keeping Your Plants Healthy

It is impossible for any book to do more than give helpful guidelines on how to care for a particular plant growing in average house conditions. Actual conditions will vary enormously, and exact watering needs, together with levels of light, temperature and humidity are all interlinked. The care that a plant needs is dictated by the way in which it grows in its natural environment. If this is understood then this section, used with the information in the A – Z and the preceding chart, will help you to provide the optimum growing conditions for plants in your own home.

How Plants Grow

Plants need to absorb a certain amount of nutrition from the soil to promote growth, but they manufacture their own food supply in their leaves by photosynthesis. This process involves carbon dioxide from the atmosphere and water from the soil being absorbed by the plant and converted into food. The essential catalyst in this process is light, which is absorbed by the green chlorophyll in the leaves. Light, carbon dioxide and water together produce the energy needed to generate the manufacture of sugar, which is either used immediately in the process of active growth or stored in the plant as starch.

Light

Photosynthesis cannot take place if there is insufficient light, water or air, and the lower the level of light, the less food will be produced. This is why most plants will naturally enter a dormant period in winter, when little, if any, growth takes place. A plant which is unnaturally deprived of any of these necessities for any length of time will become severely debilitated. This is not to say that all plants have the same needs; plants' growing cycles vary according to the climate and conditions they are naturally adapted to growing in.

How much light All plants need light but not all of them need the same amount of light. Once you know the light requirements of a particular plant, care should be taken to position it accordingly. A sun-loving plant grown in shade will develop long, weak stems and pale leaves, whereas a shade-loving plant will shrivel in bright light. Plants with variegated foliage usually need good light to sustain their colouring and will tend to revert to green if they are grown in shade. This is true of tradescantia in its variegated form, but if it is exposed to very bright sunlight the delicate colouring becomes bleached. The waxy-leaved codiaeum, by contrast, needs the maximum amount of light to bring out the full intensity of its brilliant colours.

Flowering plants need a good deal of light energy to bloom, and should never be moved from a bright spot when in flower. They will visibly strain towards the light source and thus waste all their energy, with resultant bud and flower drop.

Plants, particularly those grown on windowsills where the source of light is one-sided, should be turned at regular intervals, to encourage even growth. There are very few plants, however, which can tolerate direct midday sun at the height of summer, and water will evaporate from the compost very rapidly if plants are unprotected.

Artificial light Most plants can also be successfully grown in conditions of artificial light, provided it is the right kind of light and they have sufficient exposure to it. Because it is the strength, rather than the source, of the light which is important, 'cool' fluorescent light is the most suitable; ordinary light bulbs or spotlights generate too much heat. Planting units incorporating artificial light are readily available.

Why Plants Need Water

Plants need water for food production but they also need it to keep their own temperature at the right level. Water constantly passes out through the leaves to prevent them from overheating and is automatically replaced by the water drawn up through the plant's roots. This constant stream of water, known as the 'transpiration stream', gives soft-stemmed plants their rigidity.

Advice on watering Tap water is better avoided in hard water areas, but since this is often impractical, at least leave water in a bucket for 24 hours to give any chlorine a chance to evaporate. It is always preferable to use rainwater, or even water collected from a defrosted fridge.

Always test the compost for signs of moisture beneath the surface before watering, because overwatering is the most common cause of plant death.

Planting a young Dieffenbachia in a hydroculture unit: the roots of any houseplant are extremely fragile

Once established, a plant can survive for years with the bare minimum of attention

Always water thoroughly, and make sure the water reaches all parts of the plant. Always use tepid water rather than cold, especially in winter. A pot-bound plant will need more water than a newly-potted one.

Methods of watering The most usual method of watering is from the top, but plants with dense or easily damaged foliage, e.g. saintpaulias, cyclamens, gloxinias and calceolarias, are better watered from below. Stand pots in water to the rim and leave to soak until the surface of the compost glistens, then remove and drain the pots before returning them to the saucer.

If a plant has dried out, immerse the pot in water and leave it until bubbles no longer appear; then remove it and allow it to drain. Weigh down plastic pots to stop the compost floating out. Bear in mind that soil-less composts are particularly prone to sudden drying out.

When to water High temperatures and a dry atmosphere will mean that a plant gives out more water, and it is essential that there is always an adequate supply at the roots and in the atmosphere to replace it. Without this supply the leaf will close its pores to conserve the water still remaining in the plant, and once the pores are closed water will be unable to enter the plant for photosynthesis to take place. Food production will then cease and the plant will eventually wilt.

In cool conditions or a very humid atmosphere, plants will transpire less and consequently need less water. Excess water not needed by the plant will only create waterlogged conditions and rot the roots.

How much water There is no such thing as an average amount of water for a plant. Different plants are 'built' to survive in different conditions: cacti from hot desert regions will retain water in their leaves, as will all fleshy-leaved plants, whereas bog plants such as cyperus grow in permanently wet regions and do not retain any.

Large-leaved plants tend to lose water more rapidly because of the greater surface area of their leaves, and flowering plants need a lot of water when producing flowers. Once flowering is over, there is normally a pause before growth begins again, and less water should be given. Plants do not grow at the same rate throughout the year. They need more water when rapidly making new growth and less when they are growing more slowly or are dormant.

Self-watering devices and holiday care Watering can be controlled by self-watering containers, but if you are grouping plants together in a large container, make sure that they all have the same watering requirements.

Other methods of self-watering, as outlined below, are suitable for short holiday periods but since the supply of water cannot be varied, these methods are unsuitable for extended periods.

An automatic diffuser will slowly supply the compost with water over a period of two to three weeks. Alternatively a fibreglass wick or crêpe bandage with one end fixed into the compost and the other end in a tray of water will have the same effect.

Plants can be wrapped in damp sphagnum moss, or placed on capillary mats in a basin or bath with the tap left slowly dripping and the plug out.

A small plant wrapped and sealed in a polythene bag will survive quite happily on moisture resulting from its own respiration for at least a week.

When leaving plants for any length of time, always remove them from windowsills where they may be caught by scorching sun in summer or frost in winter.

Temperature and Humidity

Most plants will not survive in a dry, hot atmosphere for any length of time because moisture in the air is as important to them as moisture in the compost. In centrally-heated homes, dry air can be alleviated by using humidifiers over radiators, by placing pots on permanently wet pebbles, or by sinking pots in moist peat. Misting the air around plants will also increase the humidity, but this must be done frequently if it is the only method being used. Different plants need different temperatures, but most plants will survive in temperatures between 10 and 16°C (50-60°F). What is more important is to avoid wildly fluctuating temperatures, since a plant that is constantly having to adjust to variations of temperature will not thrive.

Keeping your Plants Clean

Spraying or sponging the leaves of plants is useful, not purely for cosmetic reasons, but to discourage pests and insects and to remove dust. However, avoid wetting the leaves of plants which are velvety or furry.

Leaf-shine products should be used with caution, because cans rarely tell you which plants may safely be sprayed. To be on the safe side, only tough, smooth-leaved plants should be sprayed.

Controlling Growth

Some plants need to be pruned annually to promote strong growth, but you should always follow the advice in the A – Z. The shape of a plant can be ruined by indiscriminate pruning. It is best to prune above a leaf which has a bud pointing in the direction you want the stem to grow in. Pruning will be followed by a check in growth.

Trim back plants when they are actively growing; cut back the side shoots of trailing and climbing plants to encourage the strong main growth.

Shoots bearing pale leaves, old leafless stems, plain leaves of variegated plants, dead flowers and dead leaves should all be removed promptly.

Train plants when stems are young and more flexible, but always tie them loosely to supports.

Soils

A good compost is of prime importance for pot-grown plants, which can only get out of a compost what has been put into it, unlike plants growing outside in garden soil which is balanced by natural organisms. Garden soil is not suitable for indoor plant culture as it may contain insect eggs, weeds and disease spores, and it lacks sufficient organic matter to make it porous enough for proper drainage in a confined space.

A potting compost should therefore be sterile, and have a good structure which will hold sufficient air and water to promote plant growth. John Innes is a carefully balanced, loam-based potting compost which is suitable for the majority of houseplants, and is available ready mixed from most gardening outlets. A reliable source is important because John Innes is a formulation, not a brand name, and it can therefore vary in quality.

Soil-less or peat-based composts have become increasingly popular in recent years because of the decreasing supplies of loam which have rapidly increased the price of John Innes composts. They are based on peat and sand with added chemical nutrients (buy a lime-free type for acid-loving plants).

Most plants will grow well in either medium, but some houseplants – for example bromeliads and succulents – need a specially prepared medium. The needs of these and other plant groups are all covered in separate sections of this book.

It is better to use loam-based compost for large plants; it is much heavier and helps to stabilize them. Peat-based composts, however, have a tendency to dry out very suddenly, and consequently need to be checked more frequently. Always soak this type thoroughly before potting plants up.

Top-dressing This is a method of replenishing the compost without changing the pot. Remove the top 2·5-7·5cm (1-3in) of compost and replace it with new. This method is used for mature plants in heavy containers, for a plant which resents being moved, for a freely growing plant which is not pot-bound and for replacing compost which has developed a crusty surface.

Do not feed newly potted or top-dressed plants for at least two months.

Potting on The best time for repotting is early in the growing season when the plant is vigorously sending out new roots.

The frequency of potting depends on the type of plant, its state of health and the condition of the soil. It is better to examine the root ball each year rather than to assume that the plant must be potted on annually. Young plants generally need to be potted on more regularly than mature specimens. If, when you examine the roots, they are found to be thick and solid around the edge, then the plant will need a larger pot; if they still have room to grow, replace the plant in the existing pot.

If you are changing from clay pots to plastic or plastic to clay, remember that the watering routine will be altered as a result – see the section on *Pots and Containers* (page

*Before a plant is potted on, any crocks from the old
pot should be carefully teased out of the root ball*

nearly dry, otherwise the roots will not penetrate the new mixture because there will be no reason for them to search for moisture.

FERTILIZERS

Houseplants rely on fertilizers far more than plants growing in a garden, because the nutrients available to a houseplant in compost are inevitably limited by the amount of compost and are exhausted quite soon.

A general fertilizer with a high nitrogen content is ideal for most foliage plants, but a flowering plant which is producing foliage at the expense of flowers will benefit from a fertilizer with a higher proportion of potash.

Lime-hating plants, such as azaleas, gardenias and *Grevillea robusta*, need fertilizers with ammonium sulphate which leaves an acid residue in the soil. If you grow these plants in a hard water area, they may need an occasional dose of sequestrene to prevent poor, yellowish growth (chlorosis).

Compound fertilizers come in many forms, but those which can be administered in a liquid form are preferable. These are given on a regular basis and have the advantage of being quickly cut off when the dormant period arrives; the others tend to remain in the soil for longer.

Nutrients in the form of a foliar feed are also available and are readily absorbed by the plant.

Advice on feeding The frequency of feeding will vary for each plant, and reference should be made to the A – Z section.

Never overfeed a plant, because overdoses can cause serious root damage.

Follow instructions for the exact rate of dilution.

Do not feed new plants until they have adjusted to their new surroundings. Similarly, do not feed a plant that is healthy and whose roots are not filling the pot – overstimulation results in green, limp plants. Never feed sick, wilting or dormant plants – they are unable to convert the nutrients into new growth and these will build up in the soil, causing severe root damage.

130). If potting on is necessary, use a pot one size larger than the old one; larger pots will lead to waterlogging and less vigorous top growth. A tight-fitting pot encourages flowering. Remove any damaged roots or rotten sections before repotting, and line the base of clay pots with broken crocks; this is particularly important in the case of those plants which need sharp drainage. Leave a 1·25cm (½in) gap between the compost and the top of the pot to allow for watering.

Firm the compost down gently around the plant; too much pressure will compact it and impair drainage. Water thoroughly but do not water again until the compost is

A display of flourishing plants distracts attention from a dreary view

WHAT'S WRONG?

The sooner a disorder is discovered, the easier it will be to control, so check your plants regularly – particularly the undersides of leaves and leaf/stem junctions. Frequent cleaning will prevent many pests from taking over your plants. Soapy water is often sufficient to kill pests, so although insecticides are effective, they are not always necessary. If you have to use systemic insecticides do so with caution because the plant will remain toxic for quite some time and young children or pets will be particularly vulnerable.

Always protect furniture and furnishings when spraying or, better still, spray plants outside if possible.

Most disorders are the result of poor growing conditions. If the cause is not readily diagnosed from the chart below, a quick examination of the conditions around the roots may provide the answer.

CHECKLIST
Watering: was the compost checked before rewatering; is there water in the saucer; did you use tepid water all year round?
Light: is the amount sufficient; does a windowsill catch the midday sun?
Temperature: is the plant positioned between a window and a door?
Humidity: is the air still too dry?
Fertilizer: are you 'killing by kindness', and forgetting the individual plant's needs?
Compost: has it become compacted?
Pot: is it freely draining; is the plant pot-bound?
It takes no special skill to decide that a plant is not in peak condition, but identifying the cause of its distress is not so simple. If an inspection reveals no insect pest or fungal disease, the chances are that you are over- or underwatering it, or keeping it in the wrong position

INCORRECT CARE

Symptoms	Cause	Treatment
Leaves limp and wilting with brown tips. Lower leaves stiffly curled and yellowing. Fall of most mature leaves. Flowers rapidly fading and dropping.	Not enough water	Immerse pot in bucket of water and leave until bubbling stops. Remove and drain. Do not water again until surface is dry. Trim off dead and dying leaves and if necessary remove top growth.
Weak spindly growth. Leaves pale. No buds forming on flowering plants. New leaves undersized.	Not enough light	Move to a bright position away from direct sun.
Shrivelled, generally stiffened appearance. Leaf edges curling under. Pale foliage.	Too much light	Move plant to a shadier position and avoid artificial lighting.
Spindly growth when growing in a good light in winter or spring. Leaves turning yellow; wilting of lower leaves.	Temperature too high	Move to a cooler spot but avoid draughts.
Leaves generally limp, soft or rotten. Lower leaves curled and turned yellow with brown tips. Stems mushy and dark. General leaf fall.	Too much water	Check that compost is not waterlogged and that drainage hole is free. Do not rewater until the surface has dried out. Repot if necessary.
Leaves pale and yellow. Weak growth during growing season. Yellowing of vein areas.	Lack of fertilizer	Give fertilizer more frequently but do not increase recommended dilution rate.
Rapid growth of foliage. No flowers on flowering plant.	Fertilizer with too much nitrogen	Use a fertilizer with a low nitrogen content.
Lank, pale growth. Foliage with crisp brown spots.	Overfeeding	When next watering, allow water to run freely through compost to flush through some of the excess. Reduce frequency of feeding.
Sudden leaf drop.	Extreme change in conditions	Check for draughts and avoid extremes of temperature. Remove plant from windowsill at night.
Lanky growth. Yellow leaves which do not drop on lime-hating plants.	Chlorosis (in lime-hating plants)	Water with softened water, and give sequestrene. A foliar feed will aid recovery.
Wilting of plant between waterings	Pot-bound	Repot and spray with foliar feed to hasten root penetration into new compost. Do not rewater until surface compost feels dry.
White or yellow spotting on leaves of plants with soft, hairy foliage.	Cold water on leaves	Remove damaged leaves immediately. Always mist around plant, avoiding foliage. Water from below.

DISEASES

Symptoms	Plant affected	Disease	Treatment
Stems, leaves, flower buds rotten and covered with grey mould	All soft-leaved plants, particularly begonias, cyclamen, gloxinia and saintpaulia.	Grey mould (botrytis) caused by high humidity without adequate ventilation.	Remove and destroy infected plants. Spray with benomyl or thiophanate-methyl. Avoid overwatering, overfeeding and overcrowding of plants. Keep water off leaves.
Base of cutting turns black (due to invasion of botrytis fungus).	Pelargonium cuttings.	Black leg disease caused by overwatering or over-compacted soil.	Destroy infected cuttings. Never cover with glass or polythene.
Leaves become blotchy and mottled yellow and/or flowers develop large white streaks. Growth may be stunted and distorted.	Any plant.	Virus – normally transmitted by insects.	Destroy infected plant immediately.
Powdery mass of orange-coloured spores which form rings on underside of leaves.	Pelargonium.	Rust – often caused by humidity and bad ventilation.	Very difficult to eliminate. Remove infected leaves and spray with mancozeb.
White powdery coating on stems and leaves – may spread to flowers.	Chrysanthemum in particular.	Mildew – usually caused by overwatering and too little ventilation.	Not fatal but will disfigure plants. Cut away infected parts of plant and treat with benomyl or thiophanate-methyl. Increase ventilation.
Black fungus which grows on honeydew deposits (causes stunted growth).	All plants susceptible to aphid, scale, whitefly and mealy bug.	Sooty mould.	Wipe off with damp cloth. Avoid future attacks by destroying pests.
Shrinkage and rot of seedlings at soil level (plant will eventually collapse if left untreated).	Any seedlings.	Damping-off fungi. Caused by overcrowding of seeds and/or too much water.	Remove collapsed seedlings. Move remainder to a cooler place and ventilate. Always use sterile soil.
Hard, corky growths on underside of leaves.	Any plant.	Oedema or corky scab. Caused by waterlogged compost and lack of light.	Remove and destroy badly affected plants. Move less affected plants to brighter light and reduce frequency of watering.
Yellowing and wilting of leaves, rapidly followed by plant collapse.	Succulents, begonias, palms and saintpaulia.	Root rot – fungal decay of roots caused by waterlogging.	May be possible to sever affected roots. Reduce watering.
Small brown moist spots may enlarge and merge over whole leaf.	Dracaenas and dieffenbachia.	Leaf spot, caused by damp conditions.	Remove damaged leaves and spray plant with benomyl. Keep fairly dry without misting for several weeks.
Stem or crown starting to rot.	Any soft-stemmed plant.	Crown or stem rot or basal rot, caused by overwatering, lack of ventilation and heat.	Destroy plant. Cuttings may be taken if discovered early.

PESTS

Symptoms	Plant affected	Pest	Treatment
Curling leaves. Tiny insects are visible on underside of leaves and on new shoots. Sticky honeydew deposits on leaves frequently followed by sooty-mould fungus.	All plants with soft tissues; particularly flowering plants.	Aphid – small sucking insect, usually green but may be black, red or white.	Spray or dip in warm, soapy water. Rinse in clear tepid water. Spray heavily infested plants with malathion.
Curled foliage, twisted darkened stems. Malformed flowers. Heavily infested plants will not bloom, or buds fail to open.	Cyclamen, impatiens, pelargonium, saintpaulia.	Cyclamen mite – microscopic spider-like pests, looking like a film of dust on underside of leaves. Flourishes in humid atmospheres.	Difficult to control. Remove and destroy infected foliage.
Large clusters of white insects on stems and underside of leaves. General yellowing and deformity. Sticky honeydew deposits on leaves – frequently followed by sooty-mould fungus.	Favourite plants: cacti, saintpaulia, fuchsia, coleus.	Mealy bug – oval, white, fuzzy, 6mm (¼in) long. Slow-moving, easily spotted.	Pick off by hand or with damp cloth. Wash foliage with tepid water. For heavier infestation, use soapy water. Rinse in clear tepid water. For very heavy infestation, spray with malathion.
Tiny spider webs appear and will bridge from leaf to leaf; foliage becoming mottled and yellow.	Any houseplants growing in hot/dry conditions.	Red spider mite – minute, very difficult to see with the naked eye. Flourishes in hot dry conditions.	Mist plants daily to prevent attacks. Direct spray of lukewarm water will dislodge them. For heavy infestations use derris or malathion.
Stunted, skeletal plants often covered with honeydew. Badly infested leaves turn yellow.	Hedera family.	Scales – large, brown/black, rounded with armoured body. Visibly sucks veins on undersides of leaves. Adults are immobile, but young will crawl actively over plant and spread infestation.	Spray young with malathion or diazinon. Since adults are protected by shells, swab with methylated spirits and allow to dry before dislodging.
Silvery streaks over foliage. Leaves may be transformed into skeletons. Spotted and distorted flowers.	Cyclamen, begonias, codiaeum, fuchsia, chrysanthemum.	Thrips – tiny, black, jumping insects.	Shake off and destroy with lukewarm water, or spray with pirimiphos-ethyl.
Badly infested plants have yellowing leaves which will drop. Leaves show signs of honeydew.	Begonias, fuchsia, impatiens, pelargonium.	Whitefly – tiny, white, moth-like insects on underside of leaves.	Spray with malathion until completely clear – they multiply at great speed.
Tattered, puckered and distorted leaves. Misshapen fruits.	Capsicum annuum.	Capsid bug.	Spray with malathion.

Spathiphyllum is propagated by the simple process of division

PROPAGATION

The propagation or reproduction of plants is, in most cases, quite simple in ordinary home conditions. It is also a very satisfying way of maintaining and increasing your stock of plants, and it is the only way of perpetuating a particular colour variegation. A propagator is not a necessity, but it will broaden the range of plants you can grow to include some of the more exotic species which need higher levels of humidity if they are to thrive.

PROPAGATION BY SEED

This method is ideal if you want a lot of plants and are willing to wait or if you wish to raise unique plants. Seeds do not always have to come out of packets – attractive plants can be grown from fruit pips and stones. Alternatively, seeds can be collected from your own houseplants.

Sow seeds in early spring or late summer and always follow the instructions on seed packets. Seeds have three basic demands for successful germination: moisture, air and warmth. A temperature of between 18 and 21°C (65-70°F) is ideal for most.

If the seeds are large, fill shallow pots or trays with a sterilized seed compost, gently firm it down and water thoroughly. Further watering will not be necessary until the seeds have germinated. Scatter the seed sparingly on the compost – it is most important that each seed has air and space, otherwise a fungal disease known as 'damping off' may decimate them.

Mix very fine seeds with a little fine sand to facilitate even distribution. Carefully sprinkle a little of the seed compost over large seeds, but leave fine seeds uncovered. Cover the containers with newspaper, and place a piece of glass or polythene on top. This should be reversed daily to discourage over-condensation, but do not move the containers themselves.

Remove the covers a few days after the seedlings have appeared, and keep them in a lightly shaded spot. They will be ready for transplanting after the first true leaves have appeared – the first leaves will be the seed leaves. Fill pots with a proprietary seed compost and use a blunt stick to make holes for the roots. Never transplant seedlings by pulling on their very fragile stems. Ease them out gently, holding their leaves. Firm the soil around the seedlings, but avoid compressing it. The seedlings can now be gradually hardened off and moved to their final growing positions. Sun-loving plants should be placed in bright indirect light. Water cautiously until the roots are well established.

VEGETATIVE PROPAGATION

Plants propagated vegetatively have exactly the same characteristics as the parent plant and are usually less vulnerable than plants grown from seed. Different plants require different methods, so refer to the A – Z for details concerning individual plants.

Cuttings Cuttings may be taken in several ways, but all need the following conditions to survive and develop:
– an adequate level of light, but always out of direct sun
– sufficient warmth and humidity, either by using a thermostatically controlled propagator, or by enclosing the cuttings in a polythene bag held away from the plant by three or four sticks and fastened round the pot
– careful watering. Check below the surface of the compost before watering; it may be better to mist a drooping cutting rather than giving it more water
– a rooting medium which is free-draining and sterile. Equal quantities of peat and sand, vermiculite, or a proprietary seed compost are all suitable. The plant does not need any extra food at this stage because it is too busy making roots. Hormone rooting powders are often useful for difficult cuttings, since they encourage faster root formation.

Stem cuttings This is the best method for plants with firm stems, normally taken in spring and summer when the plant is actively growing. Choose a mature shoot from the upper part of the current season's growth. If it is too young it will rot before the roots have developed and if it is too tough it will lack the vigour to root easily. Do not use stems that have flowers or flower buds. The best length for a stem cutting is between 7·5 and 15cm (3-6in).

Using a sharp knife, make a diagonal cut just below a leaf joint, or, if a heeled cutting is required, simply pull off a side shoot with a strip of bark from the main stem. Remove the lower leaves but retain the upper ones. Dip the end in hormone rooting powder and place the shoot in watered compost.

Plants can also be rooted in water. Tradescantia, saintpaulia and impatiens will all root quickly in this way, but the roots will be more fragile and extra care is needed when potting up. Place a little charcoal in the water to keep it 'sweet'.

If kept in a warm and close atmosphere most stem cuttings will root within 10-28 days. Some do take longer, so if the cutting looks healthy though there is no evidence of roots, it is worth persevering.

Leaf cuttings This method is particularly suited to fleshy-leaved plants, like *Peperomia magnoliaefolia* and plants which lack stems, for example, saintpaulia and sinningia (gloxinia) etc. For plants with smaller leaves use the whole leaf with the stalk attached. Snip the stem off as near to the base of the plant as possible, and place the stalk in the rooting medium at an angle to prevent shading the new plantlets which will shoot up from the base.

Put the pot in a polythene bag, as described above, or in a propagator at a temperature of 16-18°C (61-64°F). Separate the new plantlets by gently teasing their roots apart, and pot them up separately.

Larger-leaved plants can be propagated

Chlorophytum produces offspring galore

that each section has at least one shoot. Dust cut surfaces with a fungicide as a precaution against rotting before potting them up individually.

It is best to delay division until this becomes absolutely necessary. Plants are normally at their best when their pots are full of roots, and unnecessary division will spoil the 'full' effect.

Propagation by offsets, plantlets and runners Some plants naturally grow small plantlets on their leaves – for example, tolmiea and *Asplenium bulbiferum.* Peg the parent leaf down in the compost and the plantlet will rapidly take root; remove the parent leaf when roots are well established. Alternatively, detach the leaf and plantlet and peg it into the compost.

Plants with trailing stems, for example, *Saxifraga sarmentosa* and *Ficus pumila,* propagate as they grow by putting out roots beneath each cluster of leaves. Direct these to a compost-filled pot, and do not sever until they are growing vigorously.

Propagation by layering
Air layering This may seem to be a difficult operation, but in fact it is quite simple. It is used to make new compact plants from over-tall or leggy 'feature' plants, such as *Ficus elastica, Monstera deliciosa* and dracaenas, by forcing the plant to produce roots on its stem. At the beginning of the growing season, select healthy one- or two-year-old shoots and carefully make a diagonal slit on the shoot, no more than 60cm (2ft) from the growing tip.

Dust the wound with hormone rooting powder and pack it with sphagnum moss to prevent it from healing. Place a length of polythene sleeving around the stem to extend from about 7·5cm (3in) below the wound to just above it, and pack it thoroughly with moist sphagnum moss and secure it. Make sure it is completely airtight, or the moss will dry out.

The layering process is complete when a well-developed root system can be seen through the sleeve. Remove the packing and sever the parent stem below the new roots. Pot up the new plant and place it in

in one of two ways. The first is by cutting along all the main veins and pinning the leaf, vein side down, on the rooting medium so that all parts touch the compost. The second is by cutting the leaf into sections and placing these on the compost. Either way, roots and shoots will develop wherever the veins have been cut.

Propagation by division This is the simplest method of vegetative propagation. Plants which form clumps – for example, sansevieria, cyperus and clivia – can be

split into as many sections as there are crowns. This is best done at the start of the growing season when repotting. Remove the plant from its container and gently crumble away the compost. Carefully tease the roots apart, or cut them with a sharp knife if they are very matted. Trim away any damaged roots or rotting parts and repot sections into separate pots with a peat-based potting compost or John Innes No. 1.

Divide tubers like *Begonia tuberhybrida* by simply slicing them up when they are beginning to shoot in spring, making sure

*Above left: leaf cuttings of Begonia rex.
Like many plants, Begonia shows a
strong instinct for survival, and even
fairly small sections of leaf are all you
need to start new plants into growth*

*Above: some cuttings are hard to 'strike',
but this species, Peperomia magnoliaefolia,
is easily propagated by stem cuttings*

*Left: Sinningia, the florists' gloxinia,
is one of the plants that lends itself to
several methods of propagation. The most
successful methods are to grow new plants
from seed, or to pot up young shoots with
a piece of tuber attached*

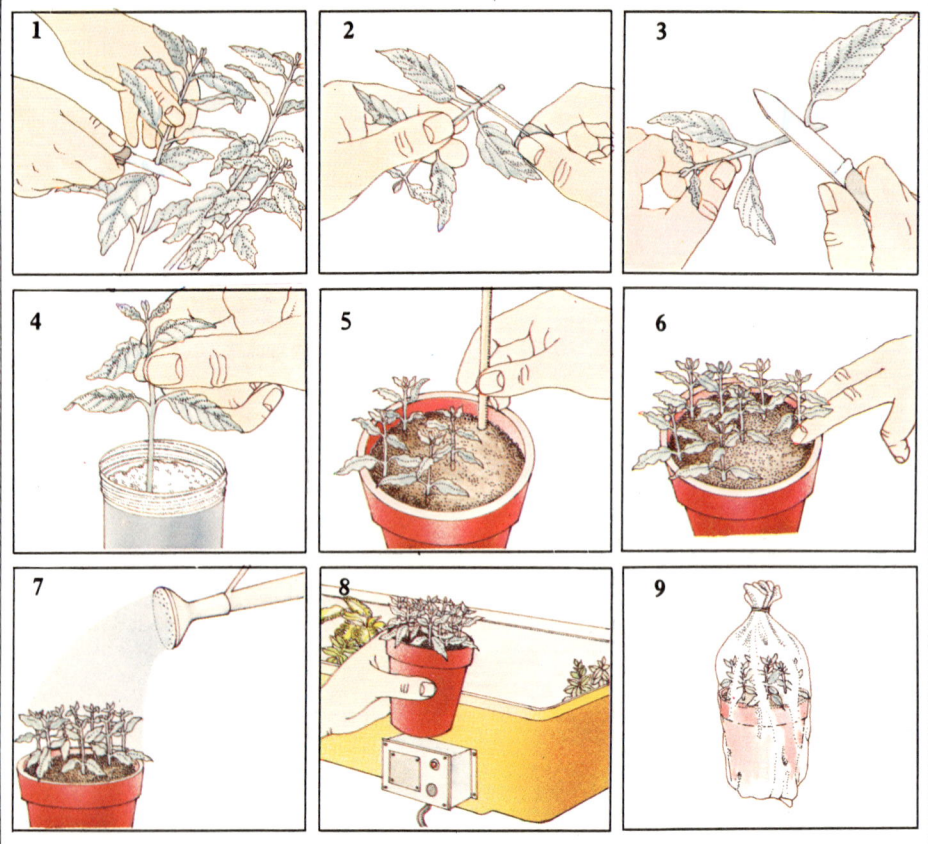

Taking a leaf bud cutting

Taking stem cuttings: 1 use a really sharp blade to cut the shoot, then 2 trim the cutting cleanly to just below a leaf joint. Cut away the lower leaves 3 close to the stem, and 4 dip the cutting in a hormone rooting powder. Make a hole 5 for each cutting, using a dibber; 6 firm the compost around them with the fingers. Water with a fine rose, 7, and protect in either a propagator 8 or a polythene bag 9.

Plants such as Begonia rex can be propagated by whole leaf cuttings: 1 and 2 remove leaf and cut the veins; 3 place cut side down on to the compost.

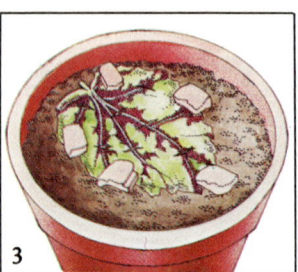

a warm position until it is well established. If the old plant is retained, it will start to grow new shoots.

Tip layering This is an ideal method for climbing plants with flexible stems, such as hedera and jasminum. New plants may take up to six months to become established, but once the initial work has been carried out the plant needs very little attention apart from watering. The method is very similar to the process by which some plants are increased in nature, where a long, flexible stem may get bent down so that the tip is in contact with the soil. Roots will then begin to emerge where the stem becomes damaged on contact with the ground – often in more than one place.

Make a small incision in one of the longest stems, or remove a small section of the bark. Lay the exposed part across the rooting medium and weigh it down. Once roots have developed, it can be cut away from the parent plant and potted on.

For notes on the propagation of bromeliads, ferns, palms and succulents see the sections on each of these.

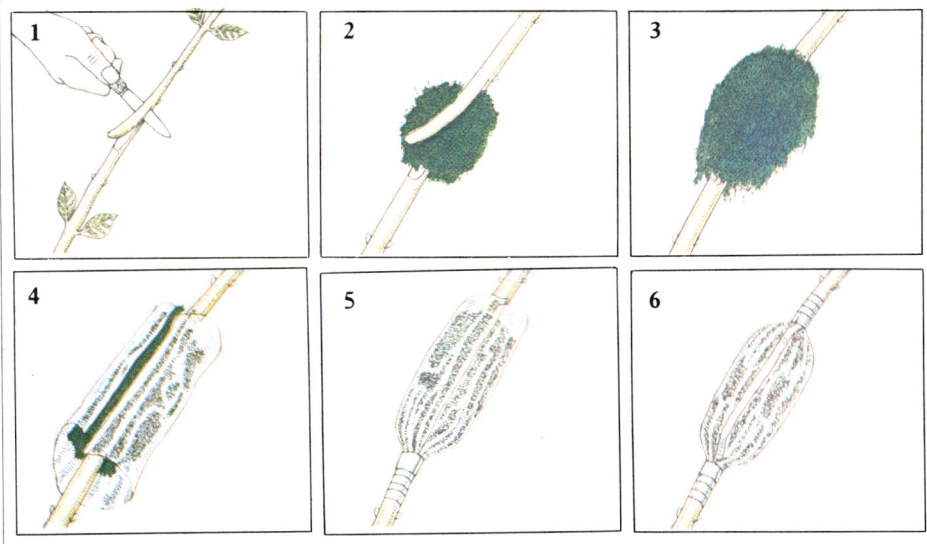

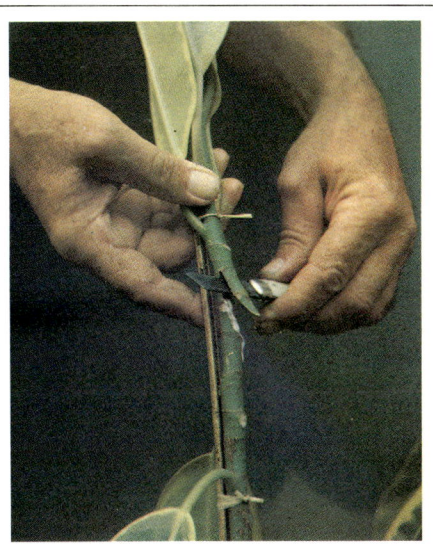

Air layering: make a diagonal cut, penetrating to half the width of the stem 1; treat the cut with hormone rooting powder and 2 insert a wedge of sphagnum moss. Build a ball of moss 3 around the cut; wrap this in a polythene sleeve 4, secure the sleeve at the lower end first 5, then at the upper end, and finally tape down the seam 6.

Leaf cuttings: for cuttings from leaf sections 1 cut the whole leaf from a plant, then 2 divide it into 5cm (2in) sections and 3 press sections top end uppermost into the rooting medium. For whole leaf cuttings, 4 cut leaves cleanly with stalk intact, and 5 insert in the compost, 6 firming the soil around them.

Above: the incision for air layering Ficus elastica, the rubber plant, should go about half way through the stem.

Below: cormlets and bulbils can be detached and potted up for the future.

POTS AND CONTAINERS

Most plants are sold in plastic pots. These have the advantage of being light, fairly indestructible, easy to clean, and, being non-porous, will retain water for longer periods of time than clay pots. Their flat bottoms also make them better suited to capillary methods of watering. Because the surface soil dries out more quickly in plastic than in clay pots, there may be a tendency to overwater them. Always check below the soil surface before rewatering, since any excess water is going to be less readily absorbed and there is the danger of plants becoming waterlogged.

Clay pots are better insulated, and are therefore safer to use near radiators; they also have the advantage of weight for balancing taller plants. Always soak clay pots for 12 hours before use, otherwise they will rapidly absorb moisture from the compost.

Clean all pots thoroughly before re-using to avoid transmitting disease.

Flower pots are measured across the top inside the rim. The sizes most frequently used are 6cm (2½in), 9cm (3½in), 12cm (5in), 18cm (7in), 20cm (8in), 25cm (10in) and 30cm (12in).

Half-pots are better for shallow rooting plants such as *Begonia semperflorens*, saintpaulia, azalea and bromeliads.

MAKING A BOTTLE GARDEN

Houseplants grown in bottle gardens can make a different but still very effective contribution to the decor of a room, and there are certain marked advantages to this form of cultivation. Glass cases restrain plants as well as containing them, so they can be useful in confined spaces and very small rooms. They provide an environment that is protected from the fluctuating temperatures and draughts of ordinary house conditions, and they recycle the water transpired by the plants, so that the overall maintenance required is minimal. A closed case keeps pests out as effectively as it keeps water in, and a plant that is free of pests and diseases when installed is likely to remain so for a good long time.

Containers for bottle gardens Almost any glass case can provide a good home for plants provided it can be closed off at the top. Large glass jars, carboys and demi-johns (such as are used for wine-making) can hold one or two specimen plants, while fish tanks offer scope for more adventurous plantings. The ambitious can make their own display cases, using sheets of glass held together by a wooden framework and sealed with silicone rubber.

If ease of maintenance is more important than variety or novelty value, choose a container with sloping shoulders and a neck wide enough to get plants through without damage to their roots and leaves. Moisture may condense on the lids of flat-topped containers, and need occasional mopping; in sloping jars any condensation will simply run down the inside. A glass dome, or bell-jar, placed over a bowl can also make an attractive bottle garden.

Bottle garden tools To keep the plants in good order you will not need more than a few improvised utensils, miniaturized versions of familiar garden implements. These can be made from bamboo sticks or lengths of wooden dowel, with everyday household articles attached: a cotton reel, cork or bung for firming compost around roots; an old fork and teaspoon for 'cultivating' the compost; a razor blade or handyman's knife blade for trimming away withered parts of plants, and a pin or piece of stiff wire for spearing any plant litter that falls on to the compost. Using a piece of rubber tube for watering should help to prevent wet compost splashing on to the sides of the glass jar.

Planting up Thoroughly wash the bottle out with detergent and rinse it well in clean

Slide a layer of shingle into a carboy, then pour the compost on top of this; the shingle makes it easier to check the water level

Drop plants one by one into the holes you have prepared for them;
the arrangement will look sparse, but will fill out in time

water before planting; it will probably be impossible to remove stains later. Cover the base of the jar with a suitable growing medium – John Innes No. 2 potting compost with some added peat and grit is ideal, or use a soil-less compost. Mix in some lumps of charcoal to keep it sweet.

Plan carefully where each plant is to go, then make a hole for the first plant, knock it out of its old pot and drop it in with the leaves rolled up for protection. Use the special tools to work it into position, then firm the compost around its roots. Make a hole for the next plant and treat this in the

same way. When planting is complete, mist the foliage. This may provide all the moisture that the plants need for several weeks or months, but if it is necessary to add more do this with great care, as the only way to remove excess water is to let it evaporate through the top of the vessel.

PLANTS FOR A BOTTLE GARDEN

Name	Height	Colour	Habit
Adiantum cuneatum 'Gracillimum'	30cm (12in)	Green	Bushy, small-leaved
Calathea makoyana	60cm (2ft)	Silvery mid-green with red-violet underside	Upright
Chamaedorea elegans	1·2m (4ft)	Green	Palm
Codiaeum variegatum	60cm (2ft)	Green variegated with yellow, red and orange	Tall, spreading
Cryptanthus acaulis	7·5cm (3in)	Soft green	Rosette
Cryptanthus fosterianus	15cm (6in)	Red and grey	Rosette
Cryptanthus roseo-pictus	7·5cm (3in)	Soft pink	Rosette
Dracaena godseffiana 'Florida Beauty'	60cm (2ft)	Green with cream spots	Shrubby
Dracaena marginata 'Variegata'	1·5m (5ft)	Green with red margin	Upright, narrow
Dracaena sanderiana	45cm (1½ft)	Grey-green and white	Upright, sturdy
Ficus pumila		Green	Trailing/creeping
Fittonia argyroneura	15cm (6in)	Green with white veins	Creeping
Fittonia argyroneura 'Minima'	2·5cm (1in)	Green with white veins	Creeping
Fittonia verschaffeltii	15cm (12in)	Green with pink veins	Creeping
Hedera helix 'Eva'		Mottled dark and light green	Trailing/climbing
Hedera helix 'Glacier'		Green and silver-grey	Trailing/climbing
Hedera helix 'Jubilee'		Gold with green margin	Trailing/climbing
Hedera helix 'Little Diamond'		Dark green with ivory margin	Trailing/climbing
Hedera helix 'Lutzii'		Yellow-green mottled	Trailing/climbing
Hedera helix 'Mini green'		Green	Trailing/climbing
Hedera helix 'Nielson'		Green	Trailing/climbing
Maranta leuconeura 'Kerchoveana'	10cm (4in)	Green, red, violet spots	Dense, spreading
Maranta leuconeura erythrophylla	15cm (6in)	Green with red veins	Upright
Pellaea rotundifolia		Green	Creeping
Peperomia caperata	25cm (10in)	Green	Upright mound
Peperomia glabella 'Variegata'	20cm (8in)	Cream and green leaf with pink stem	Trailing
Peperomia hederaefolia	15cm (6in)	Grey-green	Spreading
Peperomia magnoliaefolia 'Green Gold'	23cm (9in)	Green and yellow	Branching, shrubby
Peperomia sandersii	22cm (9in)	Silver and green bands	Dense, spreading

Some examples of established bottle gardens, using coloured chips on the soil, a powder-bowl bottle and (right) a tinted-glass carboy

Pilea cadierei 'Nana'	30cm (12in)	Green with silver patches	Compact, branching
Pteris cretica	30cm (12in)	Green and white	Upright, delicate
Sansevieria hahnii	15cm (6in)	Green, banded grey and yellow	Rosette
Scindapsus aureus 'Marble Queen'	2m (6ft)	Mainly white with green spots	Trailing/climbing

WHAT PLANTS CAN OFFER YOU

Plants can quite literally transform a room. Whether standing in solitary splendour, or grouped together in attractive containers, they have the ability to bring a room to life in a thoroughly personal, and sometimes unpredictable, way.

Certain plants have an air of formality about them. The palms, aspidistra and araucaria – with their dark leaves and erect, though totally dissimilar growing habits – are indelibly associated with the Victorian era, and can evoke a period feel in a room. The palms and aspidistra are slow-growing long-lived plants which have an air of permanence about them.

For dramatic effect on a large scale of a quite different order, the philodendrons and the Swiss cheese plant *Monstera deliciosa*, have a rampantly expensive air, and the ability to fill a space with great rapidity. Their huge, glossy leaves are best when seen uncluttered by other smaller plants or objects around them. An altogether softer and more graceful effect is given by *Ficus benjamina* with its arching stem and elegant oval leaves.

The striking outline of the dracaenas, with their bare stems, topped by tufts of narrow leaves, gives a rather exotic effect when seen in isolation from other plants, and spiky *Yucca aloifolia* looks almost futuristic in an austerely furnished room.

A plant with a naked stem will be less obtrusive in a setting than a plant like fatsia (aralia) or schefflera, whose leaves are borne on stems all the way down the plant.

The leaves themselves can have many different qualities, whether smooth or hairy, glossy or matt. The lovely house lime *Sparmannia africana* has large lime-green leaves which appear almost translucent when the light is on them and a light, airy quality very different in effect from the robust, glossy leaves of the rubber plant *Ficus elastica*.

All these plants look best grown as specimens, that is as single features, and given adequate space many will in time form small indoor trees.

SPACE

The question of how much space you have is likely to influence which plants you grow. In a small room a large-growing plant can be overwhelming, and in any case will probably look rather uncomfortable squashed into a corner. In these circumstances it is better to choose a slender plant, like *Ficus benjamina*, which, though often growing to a considerable height, will fit into a narrow space with far more ease than a large plant with a broad spreading shape, such as *Monstera deliciosa*.

SCALE

The size of the leaves themselves will also affect the scale of a space. Large-leaved plants look better in surroundings where other objects are of a similar scale. If your rooms contain many items of furniture and ornaments which are small and detailed, then choose smaller-leaved plants to complement their size.

Rhoicissus rhomboidea and *Jasminum poly-anthum* will both cover a wall or frame an arch between rooms in a couple of years, but they will give quite different effects of scale. Rhoicissus will dominate with its dark, shiny triangular leaves and exuberant tendrils, whereas jasmine will produce an infinitely more delicate effect with its tiny pointed leaves. If grown in this way jasmine is not likely to flower, but the tracery effect on a white wall is absolutely delightful.

With skill you can use scale to great effect to create different spatial illusions. You may choose to make an immediate impact in a small room by restricting yourself to two or three larger pieces of furniture and one large feature plant, or you may decide to spread the points of interest around the room by having several smaller pieces and groups of plants in different places.

The scope presented by a larger room will be apparent, and here, plants can be

Above: plants can impart a luxurious quality to otherwise rather featureless rooms. However, the ferns used here (mostly nephrolepis, with asplenium in the foreground), would need constant attention in these conditions

Left: large windows are often difficult architectural features to deal with. This arrangement of ferns and smaller potted plants helps to soften the austere outlines and give life to a geometric arrangement

*Houseplants do not always need to be at tabletop level;
place some on high shelves and others down on the ground*

used very effectively to divide a large space into different areas, either by positioning the plants singly, or by literally constructing a planted screen.

PLANTS FOR A PURPOSE

Climbers A room-divider can be made quite simply by erecting a frame of lightweight trellis, and either attaching it to the wall on one side or putting it on castors so that the whole construction can be easily moved for cleaning purposes. *Cissus antarctica*, *Rhoicissus rhomboidea*, *Philodendron scandens* or *Hedera canariensis* will all cover a screen like this fairly rapidly. And since all are tolerant of quite shaded conditions, it will not matter if they are at a distance from a window. Keep the leaves misted and wipe them with moist cotton wool from time to time to remove dust.

Syngonium podophyllum has large, arrow-shaped leaves, which look very striking when framing a large picture window. In a smaller space it is best trained on a moss pole and kept pinched out to form a short, bushy climber.

Trailers Plants whose natural habit is to trail or creep can also be used for similar purposes. Open shelves dividing, say, a kitchen from the rest of a living area can be decorated with plants like the flowering ivy-leaved geranium *Pelargonium peltatum*, tradescantia, *Saxifraga sarmentosa*, *Tolmiea menziesii*, chlorophytum and many others. Tradescantia is all too often seen with a few straggly leaves clinging tenuously to a long thread, but when it is grown properly, with its leading shoots constantly pinched out, it can make a splendid mound of satiny greenery. It looks good grown together with the variegated forms, and similar plants like zebrina and the purple-leaved setcreasea.

Hanging baskets Trailing plants grown in hanging baskets or other containers look particularly good in rooms with high ceilings, with two or three hanging at different heights. A good specimen of chlorophytum weighed down on all sides by its plantlets is hard to beat. Try growing *Asparagus*

Azalea indica provides winter colour in a formal chimney place

sprengeri one above the other in tiers of wire vegetable baskets, to produce a fountain of greenery.

Nephrolepis exaltata 'Bostoniensis' must be one of the most popular plants for a hanging basket, but there are several other ferns which look every bit as spectacular. *Davallia canariensis*, the hare's foot fern, produces an abundance of light green, feathery fronds and is actually a great deal easier to grow. It has the added attraction or curiosity of its small, furry rhizomes which creep over the surface of the container and hang down over the edge like animals' paws.

The quaint little trailing succulent *Ceropegia woodii* looks delightful grown in a small hanging pot amongst other small-leaved plants, with its tiny heart-shaped leaves threaded on long stems, and occasionally ornamented with small pinky-brown flowers.

Other plants that will flower in hanging containers include *Begonia tuberhybrida* 'Pendula', *Plectranthus oertendahli* with pale pink flowers on long stems, and the spectacular *Columnea microphylla* with trails of tiny dark green leaves and vivid red flowers – but it needs a high degree of humidity to survive.

Windows A north-facing window which gets good light but no direct sun will make a fine setting for some of the epiphytic plants. Grow the striking stag's horn fern *Platycerium bifurcatum* in a hanging basket or wired on to a piece of bark with moist sphagnum moss. *Cryptanthus* and the many other fascinating air plants (*Tillandsia*) grown in the same way can make an impressive feature of a long window if they all hang at different levels. They will need frequent misting and you must be certain that the window is completely draught-proof.

A large window can be lightly 'curtained' with climbers grown on wires or trellis fixed across. Choose plants which do not make too dense a leaf cover and obstruct your light. *Abutilon striatum thompsonii* is actually a small shrub, but its upright sparsely leaved form makes it very appropriate to this kind of display, and its large, green and yellow mottled leaves look translucent against the light.

It is not often realized that the familiar asparagus fern *Asparagus plumosus* develops into a climber in maturity and can look splendid as a frame for a shady windowsill with a collection of other ferns and shade-loving plants in the foreground.

Shelves fixed across a recessed window can make a home for a group of flowering plants, and disguise an unfortunate view at the same time. If the window is a sunny one, it is the ideal place for a collection of low-growing cacti and succulents which will not block your light.

Colour All plants are not, of course, a uniform shade of green, and a collection of entirely green-leaved plants is never a dull sight. Greens range from the bright yellow-green of the bird's nest fern to the dark grey-green of the rubber plant. And then there are the many plants with variegated and coloured foliage. These, together with the flowering plants, can be used very effectively to make splashes of colour and accentuate certain areas in a room. The

ferns and other shade and moisture-loving plants, like *Cyperus alternifolius* and *Spathiphyllum wallisii*, will create an atmosphere of lush tranquillity in a shady corner, and you might balance this by having a group of colourful coleus in a sunnier spot, or a single colourful bromeliad on a table where it will arrest attention.

The cooler white, cream and green variegated plants such as aglaonema and *Dieffenbachia picta* 'Exotica', the variegated ivies and tradescantias, and golden variegated *Scindapsus aureus* and *Dracaena godseffiana* will do much to highlight, but not overwhelm, a group of predominantly green plants.

By contrast, the 'hotter' colours of codiaeum, the zebra plant *Aphelandra squarrosa*, and some of the *Begonia rex* hybrids are better on their own without too much competition from other colours.

The more subtle striations of the lovely marantas and calatheas, the warm terracotta of *Rhoeo discolor*, and the dark red-purple of *Cordyline terminalis* 'Firebrand' are far less demanding and look well grouped together.

The breathtaking array of colours offered by the caladium hybrids with their huge, papery leaves will produce a different kind of impact from that of codiaeum, whose waxy leaves in volcanic reds, browns and yellows are equally dazzling, but more robust and down to earth.

Plants for Special Conditions

You can grow plants in just about any room in the house, but certain rooms offer special conditions that suit some plants better than others. Keep plants needing constant warmth in the main living areas, and those that prefer cooler conditions in bedrooms.

Kitchens may be subject to quite wide fluctuations of temperature, and the possible hazard of gas fumes. If the space is small, stick to the familiar indestructibles like tradescantia, chlorophytum, rhoicissus and so on. Ferns and African violets might be quite happy on a windowsill over a sink, where they will get frequent steam baths. Herbs, impatiens and pelargonium

will all grow well and look very attractive on a sunny windowsill. Bathrooms can offer humid conditions for ferns, saintpaulias and *Ficus pumila*, but only if they are kept permanently heated. If the temperature tends to plummet when the bathroom is not in use, try aspidistra or palms. Bathrooms are sometimes used as temporary convalescent homes to revive plants that are suffering from hot, dry conditions.

Halls and passages are usually distinctly cooler than other areas of the house and, provided they are relatively free of draughts, make good homes for some of the plants that prefer cool, shady conditions, such as grevillea, araucaria, aspidistra and palms. Flowering cyclamens, azaleas and *Begonia rex* will grace a hall table where there is good indirect light. And if you do not want to miss a single opportunity for decorating your house with plants, you might have *Philodendron scandens*, *Tetrastigma voinierianum* or × *Fatshedera lizei* twining up the banisters of the staircase, or hanging baskets of ivy, chlorophytum or *Asparagus sprengeri* cascading down through the stairwell.

Decoration and Function

These are just a few of the ways in which plants familiar and unfamiliar can be grown for different purposes and effects. Decoration can be made to combine with function in a number of delightful and surprising ways, but be careful not to take it too far. There is little point in moving a small tree into your home if there is not going to be room for you, your children, cats, dogs and the plant.

A deliberately overcrowded effect in a small room can be charming and very intimate, but it needs to be controlled. If you have to move several plants every time you want to open the window or get to a cupboard, then it will probably drive you mad, and the plants won't like it either.

Keep plants away from direct sources of heat such as radiators, and out of the line of draughts. You will find that if you give some thought to the welfare of your plants before you position them they will reward you in return.

Nephrolepis – an undemanding houseplant with lovely, frilly fronds

INDEX